# The JOURNEY

## DAVID GUNNIP

Quantum
Discovery
A LITERARY AGENCY

ISBN
978-1-961601-86-4 (Paperback)
978-1-961601-87-1 (eBook)
978-1-963254-07-5 (Hardcover)

# TABLE OF CONTENTS

## PART ONE

## SECOND STORY

# THE JOURNEY

## BY

## DAVID GUNNIP

Today is August 1, 2023... I was born October 16, 1952... These are my stories. Written for myself, my wife Dianne, my brother Danny, my girls, Jenna and Kate and mostly my grandchildren, Johnny and Rosie. I have watched many lives pass by with no real recollection of what actually happened to them. I, as best I can guess, didn't really care much either until Johnny was born... and then Rosie... Suddenly, realizing the limits of time, it became very important to me that they both at least could hear my recollection of the events. I have written them over these last 5 or 6 years as I remember them best, some of the people involved may remember the events differently but this is my honest version of all of these tales...

**⚫◆⚫**

# MY STORY

My Mother scared me. I guess I was three or four and don't remember much before that, but it seemed like every word out of her mouth was "you can't" or "you'll never". Well, she was wrong, but at the time it's your Mom so... we were living in Stamford, CT. on Seaside Avenue in what can only be described as the worst house in the neighborhood. Three families, run down, with a dirt front yard about 10 feet deep on a main road with cars flying by so close that if you fell forward at the wrong moment you were done. The Pisches, The Schulls and us, The Gunnips. Barb and Sandy Schull, Alison and Joanie Pische and me, little Davy Crockett (those too young to remember the "king of the wild frontier, the three Walt Disney TV shows", and "last man to die at the Alamo". Well, I had a thing for the Alamo, so if you didn't call me "Crockett" I guess I freaked out... Well these four girls were their own little gang so I got it pretty good on a regular basis... "Davy Gunnip!... Davy Gunnip!", then "BOOM' a shot to my coonskin cap and down I'd go. Four on one, even four little girls, were pretty bad odds so I started off losing a lot of fights. Later on in life I didn't lose many so I guess I have the girls to thank for that. My mother was pretty good (or not) about letting me go out by myself... at three years old... like 9:00 in the morning til 5:00 at night... every day and night. I didn't see much of her but it was a daily deal so I never thought much about it til I grew up years later. I'm not sure if she didn't want me around or just didn't know how to deal with bringing up a child. I guess when you're poor with nothing to compare it to you just roll along as best you can and take the routine for granted. My Dad was a different story. I knew he loved me. I'm not saying my Mother didn't, I just think she had no clue how to express emotions… any emotions, at least not to me. My Father worked a couple of jobs every day so I didn't get to see him much, but when I did he could make me feel like the best kid in the world. He was Irish, athletic, funny and he was… happy. Back then I can't ever remember him not smiling or joking it up. Like I said he was Irish, which meant he was a pretty good drinker, looking back I guess he was well along the way on any given day, but to a little boy, smiling down with eyes that looked at you with real love, and well, it was all I needed. Something which at the time I didn't see, but came to realize again as I grew up is where I found most of my love and life was in music. There was always music playing inside our house when my Dad was home. We had a record player and back then the music was played on a disc called a "45". One song (the hit) on one side and the "B" side, sort of another song, not heard on the radio, but I guess you got as some sort of a bonus on the flip side. We had a stack of 'em and my father would walk in the door, put the whole bunch on and play song after song til the stack was gone. Then he'd turn them over and play the other side. All kinds of music, Sinatra… Bing Crosby, Nat King Cole. But not just big band stuff, country (back then country & western), jazz… black, white… just music. One of my favorite groups were The Ink Spots. A black group, I think five guys, doing real harmony. I couldn't figure out how they did it, but I was sure I liked it the most. Anyway I knew the words to every song on both sides of every record and found myself singing almost all the time. At this point, I didn't have any real friends, so the songs became my pals. Come to think of it, they still are.

Anyway, what I thought I would do is string together the moments in my life that I remember as the most defining bits and pieces of the guy who is sitting here typing today. It's been quite a ride, both up amazing hills and down into some pretty dark valleys. If only for my two daughters… and mostly I think for my grandson, Johnny and granddaughter Rosie, recently arrived that I am writing this down. My girls have heard many of these stories along the way (not so much Johnny and Rosie) but in no order or with much, if any explanation. And I guess for me… maybe when I'm done I'll have a better grip on the why and how I have reached this moment, relatively intact, reasonably sane and mostly, yea mostly, happy. So anyway, here goes…

•••━●━━━━━●━━━━●•••

# MY DAD

A moment here now about growing up with my Dad… I didn't even know it at the time, but he was Irish. With that came some pieces of a puzzle that I still live with, still trying to rationalize, explain or lie about. It was all about sports, drinking and fighting. He was real good at all three. My first memory was at a place called the Colony Grill. I was about three and Dad pitched for the bar team, I was the batboy and after every game all the guys would go back to the bar. My deal with Dad was I got a bag of chips, a Coke and a slice of his pizza, as long as I told Mom we stayed at the field after the game, hung out there and came home. Hey, soda, chips and pizza, so I was in. They could go pretty fast back at the bar. Shots and beers… No worries… One day I was sittin at the bar with Dad and the rest of the team and some guy says "What's this kid doin' sittin at the bar?". Dad says "that's my son and mind your own business" (it might have been a little more colorful on both sides cause it escalated kinda quickly), next thing I see is my Dad knockin' this guy out with one punch. Bang!… right off the stool, right to the ground. The owner, a fella named Bo Bohanan, said "Charlie, damn it, you gotta stop knockin guys out in my bar", so I got the idea this wasn't the first time he'd been down this road. I was jaw dropped, stunned. But from that day forward I was aware that the man

I SO looked up to, who I knew loved me most, was much more than just my easy going Dad in both good and bad directions. Never forgot it.

# SEASIDE AVENUE TO WILLOWBROOK AVENUE (AGE 4 YEARS AND 10 MONTHS)

So around this time two big deals happened, I got a baby brother (Danny) and we moved to 52 Willowbrook Avenue. It was a house. No, I mean a HOUSE!! For about two weeks I had my own room… then Danny came along and I had a roommate again. Over at Seaside it was me, Mom and Dad in one room (which looking back now couldn't have been much fun for them either… ). But this was our house, just one family, one house. I felt rich. I wasn't, we weren't, but I wasn't getting beat up every day by the girls either so I was livin' large. As I see life today, this was a small house, 5 little rooms and a tiny back yard but it was my backyard. Also, the first thing I remember, the day we moved in, was a bunch of guys, friends of my Dad's, a big old truck, the box with my toys… and the record player. My father plugged it in and put the stack of 45's (old records) on and the music had followed me to my new home. It was before any furniture was in place, before any box was opened. I looked up at him and he was smiling. It was HIS house. He was a rich man. He came from nothing and he said to me, "I've never owned anything before in my life, but an old car". He was always a proud man, real popular, great athlete and an all around good guy. But this was different. He did this.

It was the summer before I started school, which will lead me to my first real "story". But not just yet... first, a little more background. I got a second hand bike. I don't even remember where or how I got it. The same "learn to ride" story we all have, but the real thing I got and in a hurry was what came with learning to ride... freedom. Up til that point at five years old, it was out to the back yard and back. Let's look back a page or two to my relationship with my Mom. Summertime, 9 in the morning, sandwich , out the door, see ya around Dave... be back for supper. We lived in an area of Stamford , (oh yeah, that's the name of our town) in an place called "The Cove". It's on the East side and sits on the coastline of Long Island Sound. If someone had planned history better this should have been prime real estate, but what it was, and still is, a lower middle class section of Stamford with a lot of row houses like ours with people on pretty much the same rung of the ladder, somewhere brushing along just above the bottom. But I had a bike. And first I rode around a corner... And then right back. By the end of the week I had gotten my brave up and I was two streets away from home. By the end of the summer I knew most of my neighborhood. This was great... never gonna end... every day, me and freedom... then...

•••◆━━━━━━━━◆━━━━━━━━◆•••

# SCHOOL

Here's the thing about surprises. Sometimes they're good… and sometimes… well… not so much. We've touched a little (or maybe more than just a little) on my Mother. I'm pretty sure raising children wasn't what she thought it would be. As I have said my Dad worked all the time so she had me to deal with. And, looking back, I have a feeling I probably own some of this relationship, or lack of one. Anyway, one morning I got up, ready to fly and I saw these strange clothes at the edge of my bed. Never saw them before… "Dave, put those clothes on". I said "Why"… she replied "We're taking a walk"… Again "Why", we'd never walked anywhere before in my long 5 years of life. I wasn't panicking but I was fairly sure something different was entering the room and my world. "Just put them on". I found myself walking with my mother, I knew where I was, I ridden these streets but I had no idea where we were going. So after a few blocks we come up to this building… I'd seen it before. Big… Red.. but always empty. Never really thought about it. This day there were people everywhere, mostly a bunch of kids, big and small. And I didn't know any of them. "Go in there', she said. "In where?"… (now I was starting to panic a little). "In there"… "What's in there?"… She didn't even really look at me, she just said "School. It's time for you to go to school". This was, I swear to God, the first time I had ever heard the word. Either she was afraid of how I'd react or she just decided this was the way to go but I was in a real state of scared now. "By myself?" I remember saying… "you'll be fine, go right through those doors." Well, I was miles away from okay but I did what I was told. I found my way to a room and a teacher and started my first day of school. It felt like prison. Kind of a bad start on the education highway. My teacher, Ms. (Miss) Reardon in looking back almost sixty years was a gem. I think she saw me clearly as lost and scared… and she tried to make me feel safe… in prison, but with a friend. Going home the first day was one long walk. I asked my Mom, "how many times do I have to go back there?" and she said " every day"… well… School and I were never going to get along, and, I guess, we never really did. But, no child should ever have to walk into a world, or a room, like I did. I'll say this. I think my Mom was scared… but so was I. So that's where we, I guess, will have to choose to leave it.

# SCHOOL (ARTIE)

Life as a kid in the Cove was all about sports. I was good at sports and once I realized I wasn't gonna pay attention in class, it was all about the playground. Out there it wasn't what you knew, it was how you played. My Dad was real good... I mean real good. He got a tryout for the Detroit Tigers as a pitcher at seventeen; and then World War II broke out. And like every other boy/man in our country he enlisted... underage. Anyway, back to sports. I was pretty good too... but there was one kid, better than me... at everything on the playground. Artie Evanchik. He was bigger, faster, stronger... and just... better. He was my first best friend. I didn't try to like him, I didn't have to. He was a force of nature, and as far as I know to this day he still is... but he liked having me around cause I was almost as good as him, so we were friends. I guess for both of us it was as good a place to start as any. He thought I was smart and I thought he was better and for us it worked well. School leveled out and now that I had my bud, well it was ok, so for Kindergarten, 1st, 2nd and 3rd grade I had Artie... and I guess he had me too. I lost Artie in the 4th grade when they decided to split up the kids according to whatever criteria defines where kids go, school wise. It was without a doubt one of the worst days of my life. I was now the best kid on the playground... when I was on the playground... but now I knew... right in my own small school there was someone better on the field, somewhere… I wonder even today how that affected what and how I would live from then on. Really… but as I'm sure is going to happen more than once during this effort, I passed what is an important moment in my story. So let me return to a day in springtime, 2nd Grade…

⊸•⊶——◆——⊷•⊸

# 2ND GRADE SCHOOL
# (MUSIC/ LYRICS )

Back to my Dad and the stack of records "45's". One particular day I was all by myself on the playground… I always sang… mostly when I was alone, but I always sang. The only songs I knew were the records my Dad played. So, I was singing… and my teacher, Miss Valuzzo, heard me and said "Dave, you should sing for "show and tell" (we did this every Friday). I'll never know to this day why that didn't bother or rattle me, but I said "OK", so I picked my favorite song, practiced, and by Friday, I was ready. It was called, "He'll have to go". Let's go back quickly to the friends I had… all sports guys, Cove kids… never heard me sing, didn't know, really didn't care. I walked up to the front of the class when it was my turn, felt pretty good… and started to sing my song. By the first line my buddies were already smiling… and not in a good way… end of the verse everybody was giggling or worse… I was in real trouble and had no idea why. But… I was gonna finish… by the bridge in the song I had picked they were into outright laughter. Not "I'm with you" laughter, more of the "is he kidding" type. I finished the song to open ridicule… walked back to the back of my class past my buds to where my teacher was sitting, past my own seat, and said "You said they would like it!?". She was somewhere between "how do I tell this child… and should I" but she smiled and said "David, you sang so well... but did you listen to the words you were singing?". Uh Oh... It was an old Jim Reeves country song... my favorite... but... the words... "Put your sweet lips a little closer to the phone, let's pretend we're together all alone, I'll tell the man to turn the juke box way down low, and you can tell your friend there with you he'll have to go... ". The bridge was worse... "You can't say the words I wanna hear while you're with another man, do you want me answer yes or know, darlin' I will understand... "Well, I was dead. And for quite awhile. Can't tell you how bad it was cause I've pretty much blocked it out. What did happen is from that moment on, for the rest of my life, I listened to every word of, not only in every song, but every important moment of my life where words mattered. It took awhile to get my creds back with the guys but eventually they grew tired of beating up on we song wise, and I got to move on.

·•••─────•─────•─────•─────•••·

# DANNY AND I

So now we enter the next really important phase of my growing up… my brother, Danny. Even if in my mind, I was no longer being seen by my Mom, I was now totally invisible. I think Danny was the moment I watched her come to life. I was Dad's. Danny was HERS. Everything became about him, don't misunderstand, I loved my brother, for real, and still do to this day, but I saw my Mom CHANGE… she cared… she actually treated me differently too. I was supposed to take care of him. I suddenly mattered cause… he mattered. We shared what for a blink of an eye was my mother… and then my room. But Danny was good. Just pure… good. I don't think he had a bad bone in his body. He was happy, he laughed, he seemed to enjoy all about growing up. I just couldn't figure him out, but I knew in my heart he saw the world , in general, better than me, and I was supposed to protect him. For the most part I did… but as is true with all children I think, there's only so much a ten year old can do. Basically there are two real stories about me and Danny that defined our childhood. The first was really bad… it was a normal summer day, lots of kids in our neighborhood; I was about 100 feet away from Danny. He was standing with a kid named Barry Stunkel. I was right next to Barry's brother Bruce. I look over and Barry is putting a… (wait this takes some explaining) back in the day there was a Yogi Bear Chocolate drink that came in a small plastic container.

Anyway, Barry's putting that plastic thing on Danny's head. But, the real problem, from 100 feet away, was the baseball bat Barry was holding. Now let's remember that Danny was (as he remains to this day) a trusting, gentle soul. Now me, from a hundred feet away... am not. I can see this unfolding faster than I can get there or stop it. I watch Barry pull the bat back, Danny with Yogi Bear on his head, and then... the swing...the obvious goal was knocking Yogi off Danny's head... but... and it still hurts, even now, he hit him right in the face. I was probably 50 feet away but even from there I knew how bad the shot was. It was an old wooden bat... not too big... but oh boy... by the time I got to him his face was already swelling up like the scene in that DeNiro film (can't remember the name), and I was sure he was dead. I grabbed the bat and Barry's brother Bruce stopped me from killing him right there. Danny, somehow, and I swear, I'll never know how, got up, but he looked so bad and I didn't know what to do but bring him home. Now comes "the why is Dave so shallow... or weak... " or just not like Danny... ( in my heart of hearts I don't believe he would've been thinking this at all)... all I'm thinking as I'm holding his nose from falling off is... She's gonna kill me... sadly... and I mean so sadly... I was right. She sees him, we get in the car and she heads for the hospital. As luck, or God would have it, however it turned out, my brother was ok. I SAW the shot. It should've killed him. But it didn't. He was swelled up for weeks, and being from a tough Irish family they got some great "boxing shots". But after it was over all I remember my Mom saying to me was "this was your fault. I told you to watch your brother". Some stuff obviously as I'm writing this... stays with you.

The second story, held a much more profound effect on both Danny and I. I guess my parents married for love... in fact I would say I'm sure of it. Years later, I read letters and poems my Dad wrote to my Mom. He did love her. But somewhere along the line they lost each other. I've always wondered if it was me. I still do. On a good note... somewhere towards the end of this story they did find each other again… First it was Jenna and the three more granddaughters… they found something that they both cherished and I believe it brought them back to each other. I truly believe this, and I also believe a life is a journey and how it ends, matters. It's not that I'm a sucker for happy endings, it's just that as I'm writing and reading this, it does appear… a little dark… anyway back into the darkness I go… Danny was maybe 4 and I was 9. My Dad had lost his main job at Conde Nast (he was a pressman, a printer on the old monstrous machines that in those days printed all the papers we read… ) I guess it was as bad as it gets for him. He lost his job and well right around here, I guess Dad had too much time on his hands and maybe that meant more drinking… Anyway, Dad and Mom started in, night after night cause he was home and out of work. Danny and I were right upstairs, but I think when you're that deep in anger, fear or hopelessness you lose sight of what is happening or who you are actually around (us). I believe this to be true cause it was happening every night. Danny and I would sit in bed and listen as it went from argue to anger to rage… almost every night… we listened from bed… and then somehow, we were both sitting on the top step… together. The last night, we were there on the steps and it was as bad as it had been. Mom said something like "fine then leave and don't ever come back!". Danny said (remember he was 5), "you've got to go down there" I was nine and didn't know what to do… But Danny was four and I was older… I heard my father say "If that's what you want… fine!!"… I remember somehow knowing I had to, and I found myself going down the stairs and seeing my Dad heading for the door, and I said "Where are you going?" Until this moment as I said earlier, I don't believe either of them were aware that we were in the same house. Time seemed to stop… Dad stopped… I was trying to be strong but I'm almost sure I was crying… didn't want to. but I'm sure there were tears. He looked down at me and walked to me, picked me up and said "I'm not going anywhere" I remember saying "You're not going anywhere!!!"… He carried me upstairs, Danny was already back in bed, I'm sure, scared stiff… but quiet. Dad said "go to sleep, everything's ok" he kissed my forehead and went downstairs. Silence… And I don't mean just then, I mean every night after, I'll never be sure why, I'm sure Danny or I will never know, but the battles stopped.

◆◆●━━━━━━━━●━━━━━━━━●◆◆

# LONG STRETCH OF NOTHING OR MAYBE EVERYTHING OF ABOUT ME TODAY

I don't know how it was for you, or anyone else for that matter, but in any story I think there are stretches of the road where not much happened… This was third grade thru sixth for me. Played sports, hung out and just sort of… was. However, some stuff did occur, (harking back to my Mom's "You'll never" state of mind) I felt a real need to "have" my own. A kid I knew wanted to give up his paper route. About 33 papers. I took it and then I took another kids route… To make a long story shorter in about six months and 4 or 5 other routes and I've got a 245 house paper route… can't do that in any day, every day so… I hired some friends and took my cut from everybody (this was an important childhood decision). Comically I won "Paperboy of the Year". Right from the start I began hoarding money. Never felt the need to spend it. Just felt like I had to "have" it. Sadly, even today, I think to a certain extent, I still do.

This leads to my next financial move in "The Cove". Lots of poor, lots of anger, apathy and lots of crime. The main street guy was a fella we called "Stingy Mingy" (pronounced "Mingie" long e, it rhymed, lets remember words, rhyme and songs were important to me now). Ming (pronounced Minj with a j) was the bookie in the neighborhood and commanded a lot of respect.

One day I'm standing outside a bar owned by a friend of my Dad's called "Robie's" and Mingy pulls up and says " Hey Davy, c'mere". He says "You wanna make some easy money" (Let's remember here, I'm 12 years old), I'm like "Yea". A little bit about Ming here... He's about 5'7" maybe 250, Fedora, and a cigar stub in his mouth literally every time I ever saw him. He drove what I believe was a big twin finned (in the back) Oldsmobile. Like I said he commanded a lot of respect in the Cove, I'm still not sure to this day how or why, but I got in his car and he drove me down to the West Side of Stamford to this liquor store where I met a black guy named Ray. Ming said "I give you an envelope, you ride it down on my bike to Ray, I pay you 5 bucks". 5 Bucks in 1964 was REAL money... I was makin some money on the paper route gig with all my guys but this was ALOT of money... So I started makin the bike ride from the Cove to the West Side a couple of times every week, hid the money in my sock drawer... (still do that to this day). I was pretty sure what I was doing was less than legal but, hey, 5 bucks is 5 bucks. This went on for quite awhile (like over a year or so) and I was livin large... takin my friends bowling, buying sodas, I was "da man". Til my mother found about $300 dollars in my sock drawer. I came in the house and my Dad said "Come up here" (uh-oh) I walked up and he had my money in his hand and said "Where'd you get this money". I gave it a shot... "Paper Route", he was pretty quick. "Bullshit, where'd you get money like this?" My Dad had a way of rolling his tongue when he was pissed and we were way passed that, (add this to the fact that I had more money than he did at this moment and this was really going to go bad if I lied) so I told my Dad about ridin' the trip to the West Side when Stingy told me to. Well, this was gonna go off the rails any way I saw it... And it did. Two days later, Mingy had told me to meet him in Robie's parking lot. My Dad was sitting in his car when Mingy pulled up to me on my bike. Let's just quickly go back to seeing my Dad knock a guy out in the Colony. This was different... this was personal. He got out of his car and walked up to Mingy, opened the door, dragged him out and beat him up… I mean no joke, Mingy wasn't up to a fight with my Dad and Dad didn't care. He hit him enough so I said "Dad, stop you're gonna kill him!". He looked at me, stopped, and then he said to him, "If you ever talk to my son again, I am gonna kill you". Pretty sure both Ming and I knew he wasn't kidding. From that moment on I knew for sure my Dad would kill for me, but also he was capable of dealing with me too, just as hard, if I stepped too far out of line. I'm now almost sure this was the moment that when each and every chance that came for me to step over that line, cause all my buds did… I didn't. It was not about the fear of getting caught or beat. It was about the fact that he would have killed FOR me. I feel exactly the same way now as a parent about my two girls today. I guess, no, I'm sure we can't stop the way life happened to each and all of us. No one can. This is just how it happened to me. Maybe it wasn't the same to other kids who then turned into parents and God knows I've no right to judge anyone, so every parent does what they think is best, but to this very day I know that was it for me and how I would handle protecting and /or teaching my kids.

◆━●━◆

# MUSIC/SPORTS

I think, no I know, my Dad's sports/drinking/fighting upbringing was never his fault. He was dealt a bad hand that I doubt I would have survived. I'm pretty sure (at least I hope) I'll talk more about his life as I write but since I'm writing this with no road map I'll guess I'll find out later. Suffice it to say at this moment, his story started with, his Mom died when he was three, he was in a youth work camp at around eight and he fought a World War at seventeen. Yeah, I'm pretty sure I would not have survived his childhood. But as with every generation, we strive to make it better for the next. He made mine as good as he could. And it was good enough. Looking back right now I can say for sure he got me to a place that I could grow, survive and fend for myself. So, anyway, Music and Sports… I mentioned my Dad' 45's on the record player and him being a pitcher on the bar team. What I didn't say was he was a great singer and probably a better ballplayer. No kidding. I would see him play ball a lot more than I got to hear him sing. On the field he was so much fun to watch. Every game mattered the most, I lived for every game, but more, I think he did too. I was good playing ball growing up, really pretty good, but looking back now, I'm willing to say he was so much better than me. It feels good to finally say that. But, I loved playing ball, any ball. I play to this day, any sport that (first, my own buds growing up and now, thankfully, the younger guys) still ask me to play.

But… Music. That would in the end define me and my heart. There are two people who made it possible. My Dad and my Music teacher in School, Ms. Genuario. Dad, at every party seemed to have a guy (no idea who he was) sitting next to him with a guitar, and they would sing and play. This guy must have been good, cause he could play any song my Dad wanted… so to me, they were good. Ms. Genuario, at school came to me one day and asked me if I liked music? I did, so I guess it was ok to tell a "teacher". I was still busy workin off the "sweet lips" debacle with the guys. So once a week or so, during lunch, she and I would sit at her piano and sing… it didn't really matter what. She taught me songs I'd never heard, like broadway or jazz, and I sang my 45's. She told me, "don't ever let your friends stop you from singing"… she knew… so started the strange and what I see now as a unique life that I am blessed to still live, and truly enjoy today, Music and Sports.

# FIGHTING

I watched my Dad fight for real a couple of times in the bars in the Cove. He never lost, and it was never close. He wasn't a big guy, maybe 170, 6 feet. But he was fast, and mostly he was sure of himself, at least that's how I saw it. In our basement (which was about 5 feet high) he'd get on his knees, we'd put on boxing gloves, and he'd let me hit him... as hard as I could. Then we'd spar as he taught me how to defend myself. He was sure I was gonna need to know how to take a punch. As it turns out, he was right. But here's the big thing, as I look back and am writing this... I lost my first fight. Well, this needs some background... Little League game, I'm 10 or 11 and I slide into a guy (Frannie Harrison) at third base hard, he drops the ball, I'm safe, he's pissed, I score and we win. So the game's over and he comes up and starts in on how I cheated. Anybody who has played ball knows that's not right. Anyway he pushes me and (just like my Dad always said, "Get the first punch in and the fights probably over") so I hit him. He went down and I was doing great... til... my Dad pulled me up off of Frannie and said, "Ok, this is gonna be a fair fight" Fair fight? It was and it was almost done! Now we're both standing up only I looking from Frannie back to my Dad and then back at Frannie... anybody who's ever been in fight knows you better pay attention to just the guy and only the guy throwin' the punches at you. So, I started getting' my butt kicked and after a few minutes,

Dad stops it and says "Ok fair fight, shake hands… " I'm now, in my own mind, beat, and beat in front of Dad. I have a feeling as I'm writing this, that at that moment it became the definition of who I would become in the Cove. Right around that time I went looking for a fight, any fight, anywhere. Not all the time. Most days were just sports and hanging with my guys. But literally at any moment where someone I cared for was threatened, I got right in front… looking back again, not so much to protect a friend, but just to prove something, again, in retrospect to myself, cause it was all about me. Sadly, that became a pattern,… all about me… it got to the point where in school some of my own really good friends walked away from me, I wasn't much fun anymore or safe to be around.

# WHAT WE USED TO CALL JUNIOR HIGH SCHOOL, AND, OH YEAH, GIRLS

Girls... Up to this point it was all about... well not girls. It was about tough or cool or... guys, not girls... I'm not sure what or exactly when it happened... her name was Joan Kaiser. She lived in Shippan... not the Cove. It was near to us but about a million miles away. Real money, big house... totally not in my league. Actually, back then, there were leagues, I guess there still are, but she looked at me and I could tell she liked me... didn't know why, and for sure, didn't care. Anyway, there was a dance, and we (this was before live bands) went together. I was good at dancing... in my room, in the mirror, to the Four Seasons, and then The Beatles... but this was a real dance, on a real dance floor. Well, in those days there was no DJ either, it was records and since that was how I was workin' it, in the mirror and I did okay. Like I said, she was out of my league in the real world... but not around... music. Real fast at the dance I saw that no guy in the room could dance, or wanted to... except me. Believe me I'm not blowing my own horn here and it came as a bigger surprise to me than anybody else in the place. But again, right at that moment it dawned on me that not just sports, but music, in all of its forms was not only available to me, but somehow, it was given to me... and to this day, believe me, I've never forgotten it, or not appreciated it. I have been blessed... that, I hope will run like one major thread through all these stories.

•••❧•————————•————————•❧•••

# MY FIRST BAND

Bruce Stunkel (Older brother of the kid who creamed my brother with the bat). Paul Adams, Jimmy Russo (we were all Cove), and Blair Schwartz (Shippan kid, but really a good guy). Bruce asked me to sing in his band. This story is short. I said yes, we did a bunch of songs that were popular than. "My Back Pages" by The Byrds, "The Last Time" and "As Tears Go By" by the Rolling Stones, "If I Needed Someone" by the Beatles., and you know 30 other songs so we could play at parties or Church dances. But here's the thing, I really knew than what I wanted to do. Sing. And than sing some more… but real fast I got that this was Bruce's band and he made all the calls. I've never been good at listening, mostly I'm still not, and I'm not saying in any way that that is a good thing, I have learned that for sure from having my own children. But here I also hit a real straight fact… all I could do was sing, which meant I needed someone else to actually play music cause you can't do it alone. So for the first time in my life I needed… or more importantly wanted. An instrument…

# GUITAR

So another very short story... I realized I needed to learn to play an instrument... I learned how to play the guitar, took some lessons, hated it (always hated stuff someone told me I had to do), but this was different, I had to do it... and nobody was telling me I had to do it, I had to do it... Me... but let's be clear, I learned just enough to get by (like always)... and I think that of myself right up to this day, I have always tried to learn on my own, sort of just to stumble along as best I could. One small step at a time is enough. As I look back now, this served me well (thank you God... ), I was just learning how to survive on my own and this may be the one of the best things I ever learned about my life, and not just on guitar.

# LYING

Writing this now, at this stage of a life, there are some really hard facts I had to face. This one is mine. If I could pull back and see myself at this time, I might have realized it and I maybe I would have been okay. But, as a child I don't think we had that luxury. All I saw was that MY reality, my truth, wasn't what the kids in Shippan had, or the Beatles, or anyone important was... so... at some point, and I honestly can't remember exactly when, I started lying... and let's be clear... it was a lie, actually a series of lies... not some whopper of a tale... they were always just a little above the bar, something believable, something that eventually I could achieve and usually did. But it was wrong, I knew it and for whatever reason, I did it anyway. I've tried to explain this to my wife, my daughter's and myself... somehow to rationalize it, but I can't. I was simply lying. I think that the reality... the truth, didn't feel fair. That may still be with me today, trying to excuse it... but I can't... my Dad used to say "you'll never forget the truth and you'll never remember a lie", I'm not sure if that was from personal experience or not, but the first time you get caught usually stops it, at least it did for me. I never really got caught, but the people around me started looking at me like "is he kidding?", and one day a guy who never really liked me, a drummer, real good drummer by the way, named Johnny Montagnese (and at this point in my life I really wanted him to like me), he just called me out. He said "you're a liar"... I will never forget it. I will never forget. It takes awhile to recover from some stuff obviously, but, at this point and very slowly, I stopped... or at least tried to stop. I think if you can't stand on the truth then you probably can't stand at all. I believe that today. I don't want to dwell on this, it's not worth yours or my time but suffice it to say I carry this weakness with me every day... every single day. Right up to this time of my life and this page.

# SPORTS/MUSIC, GIRLS AND FIGHTING, PART 2 AND THEN HIGH SCHOOL

Here comes some of the fun part… there comes a moment in life, at least mine, where you go… hey, I'm not .. y'know a loser… (big deal in the Cove), I was singing, with my guitar, playing sports on the teams in school, and I was getting better at dealing with girls… there was one bad side still…fighting. I think for some reason at that point I actually liked it. Anytime, anywhere… it mattered that they knew… don't mess with me… ever… but then something interesting happened here. I was always in the lower group, academically in school, never opened a book, didn't care… wasn't part of what I needed. I got C's in everything., didn't care… til I was going into high school. We took some test one day, didn't seem like it mattered at all, teachers didn't seem to care either, nobody warned us, it just sort of happened. Well, my life took one of it's major changes here. My Dad, (who was not talking to me much at this point, really probably, much of it totally my fault), out of nowhere says, "just talked to your teacher and she says you're smart, really smart" then he says, "she says you belong in 10A, (super smart kids, didn't know any of them and really had no interest in wanting to). I was planning on 10C or D where most of my friends were. I said "no I'm not. So my Dad says, "well, you're in 10A and if you don't pass you can't play sports".

That was it. Let's go back a bit… I had never opened a book, didn't care… but no sports?… that was real and that was harsh. I was not ready in any way to actually be a student, much less be in with a bunch of kids who really were… my whole world had revolved around the guys on the street, the teams or the girls who hung with those two groups. I will NEVER forget walking into my first 10A class. Advanced Placement Chemistry. I didn't, as a general rule, scare easily. But, I looked around at a group of STUDENTS… no nonsense, here to learn type of kids, and I was out of my depth. I think the teachers name was Mr. Dowd and anyway he started talking about how exciting the World of Chemistry was and I wanted to die… Now, here comes the thing about me… it's all about surviving… a girl in the room was sitting next to me. Her name was Linda Dardis. She was pretty, and looked really smart. You can watch folks and tell if they're comfortable in the situation, and she was… I knew I needed a world of help and I asked for it… right after class. I think she may have known me from around the halls, and for sure had NO idea what I was doing in all of her 10A classes, but I was in trouble and I think she just saw it. So, she let me be her friend, which meant both some stuff I knew I needed and some stuff that she knew I needed to learn. But I also think she needed a friend like me. Not a book guy. I think we both needed something. For me it was learning how to learn. I'll never forget she said "OK, you can look over my shoulder (cheat) but you're coming over to my house so I can teach you to do it on your own. Her Dad used to say something like " I'm getting tired of seeing this kids ass in front of my refrigerator". I'd like to think he liked me, but I'm still not sure. But Linda did. I owe her more than she'll ever know. She taught me how to learn… on my own. We're still friends to this day. She remains one of the only people who will call me out. To her, wrong is wrong, and believe me around that point in my life I was wrong a lot more than I was right. Anyway, Linda was probably the most important person in my life at a time when I needed someone to help me grow up…

actually learn to learn. I started to "pay attention" in class. I never thought I was particularly smart, (way back to the first paragraph of this story), but I (with Linda's help) started to grasp idea's, facts and philosophies being put forward in all my classes, in and with a group of students who wanted to learn. I found myself enjoying the experience. And began to do better. So... here's where the other trouble really started. See, all my friends were on the streets or on the teams and they, well, let's just say 10A Dave didn't sit to well in their wheelhouse. It was "you think you're better than me"? Or "I figured you'd be hanging out with the college kids". Can anyone tell me where it says on this God's planet that jealousy, or disdain or just plain meanness deserves a spot? You're 15 years old and suddenly you're caught between the past (which at best was tough), and a possible future (which also at best was scary or worse, beyond your abilities). So... I tried to balance these two worlds as best I could. I like to think I handled it well. Truth was I don't think I did. My old friends treated me... different, and the 10A kids had no clue who or what I was, and didn't really care, they were already grounded and on a path that either they or their parents had chosen for them. At this particular point in time my Dad and I were about to enter a personal battlefield built for two, which looking back now became, for better or for worse, an obvious defining point in who I am now.

# LEAVING HOME & STILL IN SCHOOL

Mom couldn't handle me anymore. I told you about the Paper route right? Yea, I just went back to be sure I did. Well, I was saving more money than my parents, no kidding. They were struggling, two kids, my Dad lost his job, and he had never been around much and all of a sudden he was... there. I was used to going my own way, wherever and whenever I wanted. Being in the "smart kids" gang introduced me to a whole different group of ideas. They lived in both Shippan and this really private section of town called "Wallacks Point" closer to the Cove but about a million miles away. Funny thing was, it was only like three blocks from my house, but they had a gate and a guard and everyone in there lived right on the waters of Long Island Sound. People like William Buckley (and his son Chris) and lots of others at that level. One was Betsy Barton. Her Dad had built a house right on the water and just as he finished it his doctor told him he had a condition that made it necessary for him to move to a warm, dry climate. Betsy was in college in Fairfield and stayed behind while the rest of her family moved out west. Let's remember this situation cause it will become important soon. Anyway, right about here my Dad was getting real tired of me and the way that I had lived since my childhood. The fact that he didn't get that this and that my Mom built the train remains a mystery to me, but suddenly I had a whole new set of rules and curfews that I wasn't gonna be good with. It got worse and then it got more worse. One night he was particularly pissed (looking back, I'm pretty sure it was mostly cause of the spot he was caught up in, without a job) and I had been coming in late, it was summer and I was also used to going my own way. Anyway I think I mouthed off at supper and he said " If you're not home by 10 and I mean 10… " and I left knowing from past history I shouldn't push this. Well it got to be close to 10 and I was a few blocks away, but I had made the mistake of telling my buds about it. So I got a lot of "Daddy says you gotta be home" stuff. So I waited till a little after 10 to prove I was still cool and said I was headin out… got around the corner and sprinted home. As I've already said, I'd seen my Dad in action and I didn't want any part of that. I got home maybe 10:15 or so and ran up the stairs. In our house Dad's chair was right in front of the door, so you could see his feet as you come up the stairs into the house. I knew I was in deep trouble coming in the door… just didn't know how much. I opened the door and my Dad came out of his chair and lifted me off the ground with his LEFT hand. While with his right he pulled it back, I was already (I think, though not proud to admit), crying, and pleading, cause I was sure he was gonna hit me… hard. As I said earlier, Dad had a way of rolling his tongue when he was really mad, and he was way past that. I'm up in the air, off my feet, looking at a REAL right hand and truly not up for it. My Mom came out of the kitchen screaming for him to put me down. He put me down and told me to get out of his sight, seemed like a good idea so I bolted upstairs. Let's be clear here. I was wrong, I had pushed him and myself at every opportunity, every button and up to this moment believed I was tough enough. Well, I was wrong. But hey, that never stopped me before. The next night at supper it was, as always, the four of us and dead silent. Then Dad said, "you think you can do it on your own, go ahead… ". Now, back to Betsy… that day I had told her about the night before with Dad and how I needed to "get out". Let's remember this is 1967 and rules were… quoting here, "more like guidelines". Betsy said "come stay with me", it was in no way a boy/girl deal, she was about 21 and I was 15 but she had a little guest playroom below the main house and suddenly I had a weapon in my pocket that Dad didn't know about., a place to stay. I also had a bike, money from the paper route and a real desire to prove I could go it alone. So I said "OK". I got up went upstairs, threw a bag of clothes together and walked out. He said "where are you going?" Being fifteen and not caring how much damage can actually be done I said "What do you care? You want me out, I'm out". And left. Truthfully, I was fine. I've told everyone since then (let's remember I grew up as a liar) that I never went back home. That's not true… a couple of weeks later, I was leaving practice (baseball high school team) and Dad was leaning against his car. I wanted to be strong enough to just walk… but there was a look in his eyes that I won't forget. He waited… and I walked up and he said, "how you doin?", being as tough as I could I said "I'm good, how you doin?". He said "I'm not so good, you need to come home". I think all relationships deserve a second chance and maybe we both needed one. Anyway, I came home. Looking back, that is the moment my Dad and I started to get our lifetime together back.

••◆•━━━━━━◆━━━━━━◆••

# ARTIE EVANCHIK PART TWO

Remember Artie? First schoolyard bud? Better at everything then me? I need to revisit him with a story of time and friendship. I was playing baseball for our high school team, as a sophomore (which to play varsity was a big deal, cause back then was our first year of high school) and this day we were playing Greenwich High School, always a big game in our little corner of the world. I was lucky enough to come to the plate when we were losing 1-0, guy on first base and one out, last inning. I'd like to say I ripped one through the gap but the truth was I got fooled on a great curveball and managed to just get a piece of it and hit a flair down the right field line. I hit it so bad no one was near it. I came around second base and realized I could make third. Guy on first scored and I slid into third and beat the throw. I kinda spiked the Greenwich ballplayer, caught him on the ankle. Next guy hit a deep fly ball and I tag up and score the winning run. Home game, big win, great moment. Two seniors came up to me in the locker room and said " Tonight, you're coming out for beers… " Totally cool, the big kids taking me down to Port Chester (18 years old to drink in NY (I was 16), and it was 21 in CT), so we're at a bar called Molica's and I had not really drank yet in my life (times have changed..) but I was with THE guys so I was IN… so as I'm on my third or fourth beer , and happier than I can remember… when I notice… a bunch of guys sitting over in the corner… all Greenwich High ballplayers from that day's game, including the guy I spiked at third. I was talking to a girl I had met at the bar, (who, as it turns out, was with these Greenwich guys). Well, he gets up and walks over, along with a few friends… Like 4 or 5, and all of sudden this great night starts lookin like a beating about to happen. Three of us and five or six of them. Third base comes up and says all big and bad, "you spiked me… and I think it's payback time"..I'm just getting ready for what looked like one more whipping… (as I said I had had a few), when I heard a voice behind me say" Hey Dave , these boys giving you trouble?". I turn around and there is this guy about 6'4" maybe 225 and solid rock. Hair to his shoulders, Tattoos and an attitude that crawled done his arm. I looked closer… "Artie??" I said. He smiled, winked and turned to Greenwich and said, "you boys don't really want to go there , do you?" It was still 6 on 4, but they quietly found their way back to the table. I said to Artie something like, "Where ya been, how you doin, what's goin on… ", he smiled and said, "School wasn't for me, left early and learned how to work on cars and bikes, doin pretty good… " then he said "you ok?' I said yea, I was good and he finished his beer, gave me a playful shot on the jaw and walked out the door… one of my teammates said the classic line, (for sure not the first time or the last), "who was that guy?"… THAT was Artie… I've never seen him since. But, like a first best friend, I still miss our time together right on up till now.

# WORDS AND MUSIC

Her name was Theresa Burkhardt. Smart, funny, and barely paid any attention to me. I was now firmly hanging out with the bunch of kids who were all a head smarter than me. I got by, playing the guitar and singing, and I always had sports. But I was so aware of my inability to keep up educationally, I never had to really reach before. I spent most of my life pretty much in charge… mostly cause everyone around me was so not… but this group, well they were all on board with their own personal paths and directions. But Tee, I think, liked that I played and sang and told me about a group she was in called "Sing Out Stamford" (a local offshoot of a national movement called "Up With People") which at the time was actually making headway as a nationalistic voice in a totally unpopular environment. Personally, I was way too self-absorbed to care much either way. At 15, I was more interested in Theresa, so I followed her to a Knights of Columbus hall one night just to see. Turned out, that for the next six years (I get kicked out later and really probably deserved it… ) but it truly did change my life… and almost, totally for the better. I don't really believe I had ever seen a group of people, kids, who seemed more committed to a cause. I don't know if I ever had a philosophy about my life or for that matter anyone else's. We got by. That was it. These kids were talking about… change… positive change. Belief in the goodness of mankind. Concepts way past my pay grade at this point in my life, but looking back, they were the ground that I built the way I decided to move forward in a positive way. I have, and since that time started to believe in the man next to me as opposed to fearing what darkness he might harbor. So, being Dave, I started to try and put myself into the mix of an already close and talented bunch of friends. I can be… a handful but I'm pretty sure some saw right through me. At least Johnny (Montagnese) did… but I also by this time had learned to adapt. I put what used to work for me aside and started playing on a field I had never competed on. Real, friendly… just trying to good for good's sake. (I was still lying, I can only say, out of my own insecurities and what had become a way through my life). Remember, this group was centered first around music and performing, Totally. I'm not boasting here, but I had things they needed. I could play, I could sing and that's what they did, on stages and in front of crowds. I also wanted that. The musicians were the first to be won over. Then the cast… nobody in this group really knew me but God knows I can be relentless when I want something… not proud of it, but one thing I have learned as I have been writing this, is that I, and/or probably anyone, but me for sure, are flawed. That being said, I was different than everyone else in this small dedicated band of believers and even if at that time I didn't necessarily feel their passion I did want their stage. Within a relatively short time, I managed to find my way into the inner circle of this cast of characters and in doing so became part of the best group of people I probably have ever known… from a purely decent and honest perspective. I did learn… it took a while and it only came in small lessons… like anything I have ever done, but I really did learn, these people were different, they were… good. There are many stories inside this section of my life that could easily be include in this series of stories, but mostly what happened was I started to grow up… but very slowly… I continued for many years after this to remain or fall back to, self-centered, conceited and self absorbed, but these folks at that time, kept bringing me back towards how they believed a good life should be led. I'd love to end my story here with "I lived happily ever after", anyone would, but I know and even then I think you know, when you're in the middle of a journey, well that's where you are.

---

# UP WITH PEOPLE (WHAT SHOULD HAVE BEEN AN AMAZING JOURNEY... BUT... )

We were probably one of the best local casts in the Up With People family. Our whole group were top shelf players, singers and dancers. I really don't know how or why, we just had a lot of talented kids all in the same place at a moment in time. Anyway, the National touring cast was doing a concert in Stamford, preparing for their concert in New York City and before they went on we did a quick five song set downstairs in our school cafeteria. We must have been pretty good. After their show that night the director of the cast asked, I think four or five of us to join the International Cast as soon as we graduated that summer. I personally had absolutely no plan, so this sounded like an idea that I could get behind. I was in three different casts during my history with UWP. The first one was probably the best. The second cast was without a doubt one of the worst times of my life, although it should have been the best and in the third cast, I got kicked out of due to personal anger and arrogance. The day out of high school I drove down to New Jersey with my Dad and my brother. This cast was a special group of elite players from the three National Touring Casts who were doing special shows thru the summer while the other casts had all gone home and our summer tour was amazing. During my time with the three casts I was blessed to see much of the world and while there are truly dozens of amazing stories to tell as I write and read this, I can only come to the conclusion that I was too young to appreciate what was actually happening and so they really just don't matter much in this particular piece of work. Most are just moments that happened only to me though and they were truly amazing, as were the people who I traveled with and am writing about. Except for a few... I will touch on these cause they, at least to me, moved me forward.

## DOCTOR MARTIN, LONDON & MY 18TH BIRTHDAY UWP STORY #1 STORY 19A)

We were getting free college. My folks didn't have much money so this worked out well, I think. We were an experimental experience with our six teachers out of Princeton University as we were learning classes while performing nightly in places like a high school in Lawrence, Kansas, or at Lincoln Center in NYC. I was a member of what was called the "Lead Group". It consisted of three guys, all guitar players and we sang about 60% of the vocal solos in the show. Some individually and some as a three part harmony trio. Most of the members of this cast had been together in UWP for at least 5 or six years so I was viewed I think, as an outsider, too young to be given a spotlight and not having spent the years that they had in the organization. We did have a lot of amazing talent in the show, so looking back I can see their point. I didn't make the call, that was our Director, a guy named Ralph Colwell. But what happened was I became pretty much socially placed outside the door. Lonely can be very quiet. You can be a big moment on the stage every night, but most of every day for any performer is spent off stage. For me, this, my second cast in UWP was a long stretch of road that I spent alone. Being the type of jerk that I was, and it was totally important (and I'll never know why) that nobody knew... that worked out badly for me and started about a five year spiral into depression, anxiety and overall sadness. For my part, I didn't have any experience with these emotions and keeping it all to myself took me right down the rabbit hole. I'm gonna leave this now, although it will cast a shadow over this next space of time in my story. Sorry... mostly for me... but maybe a little bit for anyone who has traveled through a similar period of time. With me. ANYWAY... This part is supposed to be about Dr. Martin, so let's get there. Well, Dr. Martin (and his wife) who were well into their 70's (she liked me and I loved her) but he was the head of the program. English, brilliant, funny, and probably the smartest and one of the best men I've ever been blessed to know. He, however, did not feel the same about me. I was years younger than anyone else in our cast (except for Johnny, one year older) did I mention he and I were traveling in the same cast together... And let's also remember he pretty much had no use for me at all. At that particular moment in time I was in a defensive stance. I was questioning everything in my classes and being a basic pain in the ass. (And believe me, to our other teachers it didn't matter). Did I mention I was not the best student?... Well, to Dr. Martin it mattered. He saw me, at least in my eyes, in less than a favorable light. We were in London, performing, I think at the U.S. Embassy (no kidding, I really have no idea where), and though not trying to be, I was, you know, an ass. But I was lonely, alone, defensive and pretty much closed off from the rest of the world, so I wasn't really paying that much attention. That night we would do our show and the President of UWP, a man named Blanton Belk, was with us, and me being a new bright spot on the team, well, it was my 18th birthday and Mr. Belk was taking the cast out to dinner to celebrate in what I'm sure was a special, well known restaurant. I remember it like I was watching someone else's life. I'm sure it was a great night, I just don't remember. What I do remember to this very day was what happened earlier in the afternoon. Our days were spent in both rehearsal and classes depending on where we were and what our teachers and the cast directors decided. That day in London, Dr. Martin's London, we were on a tour of the sights of the city. We were walking past the Tower of London and Dr. Martin was passionately giving us his knowledge of his town. So I was dragging along the back and suddenly I heard "Mr. Gunnip, do you have an opinion?" Well, since I hadn't been listening I was at a serious disadvantage so I just let the silence hang. I had rarely, no, never seen Dr. Martin angry. But he was. At me. He said "You're walking, no standing, blindly next to a wall built by the prisoners of this prison a thousand years ago. Take a look!" I did. Each square foot of the wall was, in stone, and carved out of that stone, each individual… each a separate piece of art, a personal statement from the past, as high as I could see and as far back and forth as I looked. Thousands… He said, (I'm paraphrasing cause I was reeling) "you, in my class, have argued how you are motivated, intensely involved in this world around us and we all need to be to help lead YOUR generation! And yet I watch you sulk and remove yourself from that world when it serves you. Well, young man, who are you? Which one am I to believe?" This I do remember… He said "I'm growing tired of waiting for you to choose". And he turned and walked away leaving from not just me, but the rest of the cast standing by the wall. A cast member next to me said "nice"… So… I was on my own. In London… and about as low as I thought you could get (as it turns out, I was wrong about that). I spent the rest of the day wondering exactly what Dr. Martin had asked. "Who are you?" As I said earlier the show came and went, the dinner past and we were heading back to the hotel (we almost never stayed in hotels, we usually stayed with families in the communities where we were playing), and as we were walking Mrs. Martin was suddenly there next to me. "I think you had a bad day", she said. It was my birthday, I was just part of a very important performance, and I was the focus of a birthday dinner given by the leader of the organization I was a part of. "Yep", I said, "pretty bad". And then she said, "David, my husband is hardest on the people he cares the most about and those who he feels are worth the effort". I'll never forget that. Or what I said next. "then he must love me"… I was not trying to be funny, swear to God, but she laughed, and for a woman in her mid-seventies, traveling the world with us, her laughter was musical and it was like water in a desert to me. She said "Dear boy, you're 18 years old, don't be so hard on yourself, it's not worth it. Life is far too short". Writing this now at my current age… boy oh boy…

## LONDON;
## PART TWO (STORY #19B)

My second London experience was life changing looking back on it in the long run and let's remember Johnny's feelings toward me. On this trip we were, I believe, playing at an American diplomatic event. We were free during that day and Johnny had formed a group of the cast to go somewhere together and never even glanced at me as they walked away. Johnny, being a year older had been in this cast the year before and was much closer to them than I was. So I was alone on a London street. They had given us a list of possible things of interest. One of these was a lecture at a school named Emory College The lecture was titled "Weaving Fantasy and Reality to Enhance or Improve (not sure which) Reality". I asked a policeman if we were near this school. He said I was only about three blocks from the campus. So I walked to Emory, asked about the lecture and was pointed towards the Student Union where it was scheduled. I walked into a large room with kids literally hanging from the ceiling. It was packed! I started this experience at the back of the room as a very old man took the stage to a standing ovation. As this obviously brilliant man began speaking, I slowly snuck my way closer. There were no seats, so I ended up sitting on the front step. I had never in my lifetime heard anyone speak so elegantly mixing humor, and amazing stories, and wisdom that had come from an obviously amazing life and mind. He talked for well over an hour and left to what I can only describe as thundering applause!!! I turned to the student next to me and asked "Who was that?" He looked at me like the fool I'm sure I appeared to be. He stared in disbelief and I said "I'm sorry I am visiting from America". He reached into his backpack and pulled out of a paperback and said "That man was J.R.R. Tolkien"... no idea who he was. He then handed me the book and said "This is called The Hobbit, after this, go read The Lord of The Rings. You just listened to the greatest writer of this century". I read the book in maybe a day, I'm truly not sure. I then bought a copy of The Lord of The Rings. I had never read anything like it. He passed away about a year later but I have read his work every year for at least 17 or 18 years up to that point in life. (My daughter Jenna was born around then and time got a little less accessible). Whenever I was reading his work my own attitude towards life changed. I'm not sure how to explain it, but I viewed the world in a different way. I realized there was so much I didn't know and probably never would. And it was okay. I lost a great deal of the self-absorbed side of me and how I personally viewed the world and my place in it. Let just leave this here as I started this particular story... a life changing experience. I mentioned earlier there were two stories that stood out in what was, or at least, should have been, the most amazing time in my life. Thinking back, there were dozens of tales, but time and space being the language of the day, these are the two I picked. Dr. Martin and I spent the rest of our year building me back up. He did. I was along for the ride but just like back in high school with Linda, I had started to learn. Not so much about how to learn, but about... Why... I was still alone and unhappy, but he made me feel like I was capable of more... so on we went. I will ALWAYS be eternally grateful to him and to his beautiful wife.

●●◄●━━━━━●━━━━━●►●●

# THE WHITE HOUSE, BOB HOPE & ME, UWP STORY #2

This next story however is as my folks used to say, is a doozy! It needs a little background but if you've stuck with me this far, stay at least for this. At this point UWP had three large international traveling casts and one special small group created almost like a rock group were called the "Smithfields" led by a guy named Frank Fields and his partner Dick Smith. Frank was by far the most prolific writer that UWP had. We all did his songs, and they were REAL good. But again that group was small in numbers. Maybe 10 kids in the whole show. Guitar, bass, drums, keyboards and three horns, with three great girls who danced and sang… really well. And as I said, these guys were good. They did all the real big UWP venues that year. So, for our cast, we were in like, St Louis, or somewhere in the Mid West and Ralph (our director) calls me out of rehearsal and says, "We need you to go to Washington for a special show" and I'm thinking, ok what's going on… Being so word wise I said something like "Huh". And he tells me the Smithfields are performing at the White House in three weeks and they want the group to be bigger than their current cast and wanted me, along with about 10 other kids from the other casts to join them as dancers/singers to add to the show and we would be rehearsing for two weeks to prepare for the biggest moment in UWP history. At the time the President was Richard Nixon and the occasion was the "Governor's Conference on Youth" and we were invited because we had been touring America's colleges and supposedly had a solid read on what our generation was thinking. I think we were also seen as a right wing, safe spokespersons for what President Nixon wanted to hear from our age group regarding how popular he and the Vietnam War were going and with all our Governor's there we were the perfect fit to say all the right things. Probably,... except for me... (more in a moment). Oh yea, the main act of the evening was Bob Hope. No kidding... Bob Hope. So, there are two stories going on here. I see it now as a real live major crossroad in my life. Part of it was amazing, beyond belief, and the other was just one of many times in my life where I did not do what was the "smart" thing to do. We were told and I mean WE WERE TOLD to say the college campuses across America were totally behind the President and his policies regarding the war and the overall sense of trust felt towards our government. Well, those of us who lived it all back then and saw it first hand know that wasn't true. But that's what we were told. Let's start by saying we walked into The White House! Treated like gold. I can only say it was amazing all day long. We were rehearsing during the afternoon at the White House for the evening's performance in the East Room and there were lots of people around. One was a reporter who turned out to be from The Washington Post asked me on a break if I thought the people of my generation were behind the administration regarding these issues. Let's remember here... it was, well, me. I now know what off or on the records mean. We were just talking, and I said " No, we've played dozens of shows around the land and they want this country out of Vietnam and for our government to be honest with the American People". In my defense, I had never talked to a reporter at this level and to this day I'm not even sure he told me of his position. None of this mattered that day but we'll revisit this the day after our night at the White House and what I believe was the beginning of the end of my time traveling with UWP. But enough about my imminent demise. The real wonder of this story cannot EVER be touched by that. Ever. So, it's the afternoon rehearsal and as we're finishing up our run thru for the evening and in walked Bob Hope. It's 1971 and I'll bet he's (and I'm guessing) probably mid to late sixties but he looked about a hundred years old. I'll never forget it. He looked OLD, OLD. He was there to learn a dance we would do together at the end of the evening during the encore that we would do when we came back onstage after his part of the performance to finish the evening. I was chosen to teach Mr. Hope the dance. It was not an easy dance. It was in a song we did called "The World is Your Hometown" and it was a shuffle step that took me all week to learn. I said "Mr. Hope, this is gonna be pretty hard to learn fast". He looked at me like I was… well, he looked at me and said "Show me the dance, son,"So, I did and he had it down in minutes… cold. And here's where the story gets good. I was really amazed, I mean really amazed. I think I said something like "Wow". (pretty good comeback, I know..) He turns to me and smiles and says "I'll bet you five bucks tonight when we do the song I'll get it right and you won't" smiles again and winks at me. It was great. I said "bet". Well, a moment later he was gone and I was still shaking minutes later. The rest of the day was a blur. Dinner in some wonderful room, a green room prior to the show where everyone was clearly nervous. More than that I think (at least for me), scared. I mean I'd played that year in high school auditoriums and some of the largest venues in many of the major cities in our country. But this was The White House… The President… (I, was not a big fan of Mr. Nixon, but still) The Governor's, Reagan, Rockefeller, Wallace their wives, and all the rest of the governer's and guests from theater, sports and politics all assembled to discuss the situation with the youth movement currently growing in momentum (we'll get back to my big mouth). So the day moves on and finally it's time for us to perform. Really one of those moments you never forget. Our part of the show went great. I thought for two weeks of rehearsal we did as good a job as you could hope for. The audience was wonderful, receptive and by the end, standing and applauding! We left on a tremendous high. As we were leaving the East room into the hallway walking towards us was Mr. Hope. Remember how old I thought he looked in the afternoon for rehearsal? Well, THIS guy looked 50 years younger! This WAS Bob Hope! He walked by, swear to God, gave me a wink, and walked onto a stage that he owned from his entrance into the room! But he'd been here a thousand times before... we were allowed to watch from the corridor cause we were coming back on at the end of his part of the evening and he killed it! Democrat, Republican it didn't matter he was and there's no other way to say it... Bob Hope. So he finishes and calls us up to do the closing number. From the moment we walked back in the room his eyes were on me. I hope I'm wasn't imagining it but all this time later I can honestly say I'm sure I wasn't. I know he liked me, I could tell that afternoon. But this was the real thing and I was about to learn a lesson, an invaluable lesson, actually. We came up to do the song and he was standing right next to me in front. He says without even looking at me, "Five bucks" and I said, "yep". We started the song and things were going great as we approached the guitar solo, played while we did the dance. It all started good but I honestly believe he threw me off. Not by doing anything wrong, and in no way with bad intent, he just added a flourish, a slight flair to the exact part I had taught him that day, never missing a step, but I saw it, lost my focus and suddenly I was behind the step and... OFF... not so much that anyone in the audience would ever know but I knew... and mostly HE knew. We finished the song, the President, Vice President, and the Governor's loved the night and so did we. I had moments with the President, Governor's Reagan, and Rockefeller and many others that I will always remember, but I did have just one special exchange with Mr. Hope that remains to this day one of those special moments in my life.

He actually walked up to me as everyone was milling around after the performance. I saw him coming and I smiled and said "You got me", and he did smile back and said, "Yea, I've been doing this awhile and it was good to have some fun with you", then he said (never forget) "you okay" and I said "Yes sir, and thanks", he winked again, turned and left my life. I was blessed to have had a day with an American Hero. I think what I may have lacked was poise under pressure, or I was just a kid out of his element that he had some fun with that day. But what I took away from that one very special day with someone who had lived such a life was "poise under pressure". Now, I went to bed in a state of emotions beyond all and /or any I had experienced before. Really don't think I slept at all. The next day... well, stuff happened. We were up very late and didn't have any obligations til well after noon. However, but by that time the daily Washington papers had all been long in the public eye and everyone had covered "The Governor's Conference on Youth at The White House" describing it as a successful social evening and an overall good time. Except... for one paragraph. "An unnamed source, a member of the touring cast of The Musical Group "Up With People" was quoted as saying that the college level youth in America were "totally against the President's stance on Vietnam and his overall direction of American Policy". Now, I don't remember exactly what I said (I never do, I mean like the next day... but, it sounded like me... and it was... ) We gathered in some room on some campus outside Washington and Ralph, our director referred to the article and said something like " I'm not going to ask who said this, I just want to say how disappointed I am and this is not the UWP position on The President or his policies and I have already made that statement to the national news media". Now, here's the deal... I was the only left side kid in the cast, everybody else had been there for years and would never, ever not do as told. So without him saying it, it was me... which is actually ok, cause it was, and I was not thrown out that day. Looking back, I think it's cause they still thought they needed me back in my own cast so why throw away a temporary valuable piece till you don't need it. So we all parted ways back to our own casts having shared what I'm sure will be remembered as one of those amazing moments in a life, if you're lucky enough to have been a part of such a day. It was close to the end of the tour and we would all be going home soon and I was pretty sure I wouldn't be asked back. Strange as UWP was, instead, I was asked to join a new special group being formed much like the "Smithfields" from the year before. All of my friends from back home (like six or seven kids) had been accepted to the UWP in the same College Cast that I had spent the last year with and I had been lonely throughout my time in UWP for so long that I wanted to be with them rather than be a part of another group of folks older than me no matter how cool that tour was going to be and I think I was just tired of being alone. So I turned them down and asked to lead the College Cast. They weren't happy but again I think they saw me as an asset so they let me join my friends. Went home for about a month before the new season started and when it came time to go I was actually looking forward to it. I didn't say much about the cast from the previous year. They were all "lifers" having been with UWP since it's inception, like 1966, and it was now mid 1970 and the command structure of UWP I guess, decided it was time to let them go. Our last city was Philadelphia and a couple of days before the end of the tour, casually everyone was told they had to "reapply" for next year. I'll never forget the looks on a lot of faces in the room. Sure enough the next day envelopes were handed out right before our last concert. Everyone but Johnny, me and the Stage Manager of our cast, a guy named Stony Burke. They decided they still needed us... I watched people who dedicated their lives to a cause, a cause by the way I never really cared that much about, just dismissed. I was there to sing, which I did love. I know now, (though I didn't then) that I came back to the new cast with an attitude that was not going to work out well for me. Uh-oh...

# STORY #21

•••◆◆◆————————◆————————◆◆◆•••

# DOWNHILL...

From day one of rehearsal's I could sense a tightening of rules. The Director's wanted to establish discipline from the very beginning with this new group of kids. Except... well, me. I was the lead member of this newest group, but I was mostly carrying collateral damage from the previous two casts and Ralph Colwell and a guy named John Parker, a fella I didn't know before, who came out of the home office of UWP quickly saw how toxic I was to their plan for this new year and new rules even though I going to lead in the show, well, I had to go. Let's remember, about me, I mean... me, I was still not yet 20 and did not believe for a second that I was in any danger of not being allowed to voice my opinion regarding how this group was being led. Well, as has been the case in much of my life, I was wrong. And I will also say to their credit, I was warned. They said more than a few times I needed to help "lead in the direction we are going". But, again at that time in my life , (have you met me yet??) especially at 20 years old, having what had happened to me in UWP, from London, to performing at Lincoln Center, or God, to The White House, I was pretty sure I was bullet-proof. Sooo... One day, right before we were to leave for Belgium to start the tour somebody came up to me and said "Ralph needs to see you outside". I didn't think much about it, Ralph and I were meeting daily on how the stage show was coming together. I came out of the auditorium and saw Ralph, John Parker and Frank Fields. Frank, who really did like me, we got along great during our time preparing for the White House, but… he was standing back behind the others and from the look in his eyes I knew this was going to go in a direction I was not expecting. Ralph, who I actually will give credit for standing up, I'm fairly sure it was John Parker who made the call but lacked the guts to pull the trigger, stood back behind Ralph. "Dave, we can't have someone leading this cast, who is not on board with the direction that UWP is going. We have to let you go… ". I didn't believe it and tried to change their decision but still sort of knew it was coming as I was hearing it and I still couldn't process what was actually happening. I said "I need to say goodbye to the cast" and Ralph said "No we can't do that". I said something like "well I'm gonna and anyone who tries to stop me will end up on the ground". No one spoke up so I assumed we wouldn't be fighting before I left. I walked back into the room and asked for everyone's attention. After having spent almost two months with all these new kids, I had developed strong relationships with most of the cast and I needed to let them know what I felt and how it differed from this group of director's concept of the coming year and the level of control it would strap on their lives and the overall experience. Plus I had friends, lifelong friends in the cast. I said I was being asked to leave because I represented a different vision of what UWP was and that the powers that be had decided to let me go. I also said that they were all chosen for their unique talents and to embrace the same opportunities that I had enjoyed… (I wanted to say more but… ). I remember leaving to applause and I think mostly shock from the cast, but their lives weren't changing so I'm fairly sure they were over it quickly. Now for me, life changed on a dime… we were rehearsing for the upcoming tour about an hour from my parents home and the fella who had driven the big rig for all of my last year's tour had to drive me home. We didn't really talk as I remember, what would he say… I was (as I have guess I have always been, re-evaluating my situation). Basically, I was in real trouble.

One moment, I was in a college program with Dr. Martin and his core of Princeton professors and suddenly, here it was August and I was heading to my parents house with no plan. No college, job or direction... I can still see my parents as I walked into the backyard, at first thinking this was some sort of a surprise visit, and then slowly realizing that something was very wrong. As I think I've said before in writing these stories down, I started doing this after the birth of my grandson, Johnny so he'd know the stories and overall it's been fun writing. This stretch of the road, from the end of the previous story and into this one has been harder to write. A lot harder and less fun, and since I know what's up ahead I have a way to go on before it gets better, but for Johnny and now Rosie along with anyone else who may have come this far I promise it does, but like in any story there are points when the darkness can seem overwhelming... and well, here it was. So, I was at my folks house without a plan. I thought I had to get into a school fast. Living back home was not an option. Also my parents weren't expecting to have to pay for anything, I had been getting a free ride education-wise and this was not part of their plan either. Western Connecticut State University was the closest school to Stamford but it was mid August. I called the Dean of the school, made an appointment, went up there, told my story, and he decided to let me in. It was the one semester of college my parents paid for and I had no intention of staying there for long. I was gonna try and move through this quickly because I thought very little of the consequence would happen. But, one thing that did happen was that I played at a campus coffee house open mike deal. I had always either been in a band or part of a large stage show. I had never played solo. It went well. I suddenly saw a small light inside the tunnel I was currently in. My search for a school turned towards NYC and a place where music was a part of the landscape and a place where I could regain my footing. I really had no concept on the size of New York. I found Fordham University in the Bronx when I probably should have been looking for something in Manhattan. But Fordham read my resume both in my history with UWP and my high school resume in sports and the academic advisor put up what was basically a free ride and it was by far the best chance I had to move forward in a way I saw as getting back on my own personal ground. But, what has always been a weakness in my decision making process remained and I moved too quickly and took their offer without even researching where I was going. Fordham is basically on a small island in the Bronx with the Bronx Zoo and the Botanical Gardens surrounded by the real world… I mean the REAL world. Poverty, crime and danger… The Bronx.. And here's what was worse. Personally, I had lost something vital to my basic core. I had always believed if you pushed hard enough towards what you wanted or believed in it you could make it happen. It had worked for me my whole life and I came to trust and lean on it heavily, maybe, no, definitely too much. Getting thrown out of UWP, not by people who had not shared the journey or the stage with me but by a group of the "leadership" of the organization who decided I was a political liability towards their vision of their own personal toy. Later in this story I will be talking about the "land of misfits and broken toys". This was my first experience with being on the other side of a bad choice and as one of the "toys" being tossed. But, looking back, and make no mistake, I HAD lost something. I came to the Rose Hill campus alone and unsure. I was roomed a block off campus with a black jazz saxophone player who was taking one class just so he could get a room he could afford. He played every night, no idea where, we probably said less than 500 words to each other the whole time I was there. He came in at 6 in the morning, slept all day and left right when I was coming back from class, but more than that, he made it clear he didn't like me, or white people. I had grown up in the Cove, played all kinds of ball with every ethnic group in America and can truly say I was not, or am not to this day, a prejudiced soul. It just never occurred to me. But I saw it first hand… at me. That, and whatever it was in myself I had lost, sent me into a downward spiral and I couldn't seem to find a foothold to stop it. My self confidence was gone, I questioned whether everything else I had done in my life up to this point was just either dumb luck or actually something else. Fordham, which I didn't know, was much more a commuter school than a live in campus. As each day went by, I became more aware of my brand new talent, an inability to meet people and make friends. I wandered through classes and walked in and out of the Student Union and it seemed like everyone else was heading somewhere, and in a hurry... except me. I thought hard as to what was wrong, or different, but all I knew was I just wasn't the same guy anymore. Nothing had changed, but in reality, everything had. I think life is all about perception. Especially personal perception. I no longer believed in me. And it just got worse, with each passing day I drew further inward away from the rest of the world. I stopped going to one class completely cause the teacher lost my interest totally. I spent day after day trying to figure out how I ended up in such a spot. And still it got worse. After a couple of months I truly couldn't tell up from down or right from wrong. I was, really for the first time in my life, lonely... I mean, all alone lonely. I'm not trying to say being so high up in a lifetime can make being so down worse, but it sure didn't help. Finally, one night I started thinking, "why"? Let's go back again for a minute. No one knows now more than me , looking back, how wrong I was, but at that moment, all alone in the Bronx, I had lost all perspective. I lived on the fifth floor of a building just off campus and walked to the window and thought, "I had a great time, but it's gone and I don't want this to go on... " or something like that. I looked out on the emptiness of the city and opened the window... stepped outside, we had a ledge you could actually stand on... and I did. If I lost my balance I would fall, but I was out there on my own, choosing. For awhile. I don't think I was scared. Just lost. I've thought back a lot to this moment. For some reason right then I thought about my Dad. I'll have to look back in this story to see if I've mentioned this earlier, but he always used to say, "if you don't quit, they can't beat you". It also occurred to me right then that his life had been so much harder than mine, beyond belief harder, and he never quit. I'm not trying to be funny right now but the next thing that happened probably saved my life. I stepped off the ledge, went to the phone and called home. My Dad answered and I said, "I need you to come get me", and he said, "right now?", and I said, "yeah", and his reply was... ready... "it's my bowling night... ", don't ask me why but I truly believe that moment was when I started to regain perspective... Finally. I swear, I smiled but still said "Dad, I've been standing out on the ledge of my apartment and I really need you to come get me... ". He got it. I know he never expected to hear this from me because we had been through a lot, me pushing him every chance, just to prove I was good on my own, didn't need him. Not at all... He had a Dodge Charger, the pride of his life, it represented things in his life he had accomplished. The car was fast, I know I had tried it. He said, "stay off the ledge, I'll be there in 15 minutes", he was in Stamford, I was in the Bronx. You can't do that. I had that car up to 100 miles an hour once, you know... just to see. I looked at the clock when I hung up. It was 6:18. At 6:36 I heard a car tear around the corner and pull up to the building. I was looking at the clock from 6:33 on. No way he was there. But he was. Swear to God. I came downstairs and got in the car, he said "you okay?', and I said "Nope". He was quiet for a long moment, and said, "that's okay, you will be... let's go home". I don't think any words I ever heard in my life sounded better to me, again, Swear to God.

•••◦━━━━━━━━━━•━━━━━━━━━━◦•••

# BOUNCING ALONG THE BOTTOM

It didn't get better fast. In fact, for awhile it didn't get better at all. My Dad gave me his car and said, "you're going to finish what you started". So three days a week I drove down to the Bronx and finished college. The loneliness seemed to follow me like a cloud. But, I kept my head down and walked forward. Believe me, I'm not trying to glorify this particular point in time, I was simply trying to survive it. I did. I did finish. The real question was, now what? I've not mentioned my extended family in this story. Looking back there are only a few cousins who have survived the ride. They are good people who have raised their own families and survived, I guess like me. Most of my cousins are gone. I really wasn't joking when I said it was a tough ride. One cousin in particular who is gone as I write this down is a major part of my next part of this complex little puzzle point at this moment in my life. Rick Nafey. My mother's sister's son. He was the oldest sibling on my mom's side of the family. We weren't close, I mean we were cousins but seriously, we were not close. After my time at Fordham I found myself back in Stamford again with no plan. Rick had a band that was really popular locally and was playing regularly in the area. I went out to see him and his band play and he said, "come on over and play me some songs. He knew what I had been doing and I'm pretty sure he also knew the situation I was now in. I came to his house on Turn of River Road, which I didn't know at the time but what turned out to be an island for me in the middle of this particular storm. I had left, looking back now, a basically squeaky clean group of people in UWP, all good people to be sure, but jaded in a way, myself included, that blinded us all to the real world. Well, Ricky and his gang, were… not. These guys were the real deal of 1972, free wheelin, raw music and any other broken rules you might choose to break and then write about proudly afterward. I went to the house for a rehearsal and Ricky said, "play us a song of yours". My stuff was so far off from the music these guys were playing that I didn't think it had a place in the room. I had written a couple of songs that were post-UWP kind of country-rock tunes so I tried them. The guys in the band looked beyond bored… But Ricky… he said let's do this one. The band thought I was a rube… but Ricky stayed on message and by the end of the day we had three songs of mine done and he said" We'll bring you out Saturday and see how it goes". Well, it went well… Outdoor concert, good crowd and they were there to see Stillwater (his band), but when Ricky brought me out as "family" they gave me a chance. Crowd really seemed to like it. I still think the rest of the band was pissed but Ricky wasn't. He said, "you got something, it's not what we do, but I'll keep bringing you out til you find what you're looking for". I'll owe him for that all my life. He let me land back on the ground and helped me find my footing. I actually moved into the house where it was all happening on Turn of River Road. Dom Costanza the Keyboard player in the band built a studio and this became the center of our lives for the next decade. Stillwater came and went and what happened next defined an important piece affecting the rest of my life…

## STORY #23

•••◦•━━━━━•━━━━━•◦•••

# MALCOLM AND THEN...

I went into NYC to buy my first great guitar. I'd had guitars and played some good ones, but I finally had the money to buy a great one. A Martin. Manny's Music. 48th Street, home of all music for instruments in the city. Got on the train to head home and sitting across from me was this beautiful blonde haired girl... We were the only two people on that train car She was strong. You could just tell. She smiled with that no "games" smile in her eyes and said "musician?". I badly tried to recover and tell my story and why I was there at that moment, and she just said "play me a song". With that smile... So I did... and to make a long story short (among already so many long ones) we spent a relatively long period of time together. Her name was Barbara Derecktor and she becomes a very important part in the next direction in my life. She was a dancer, daughter of a fella named Bob Derecktor who was the last great wooden yacht boat builder of our time, as I've been told, had a place in Mamaroneck called Derecktor's Boatyard. One of many Dad's in a long line who would loathe me for different and or obvious reasons... But Barbara... she just "sparkled" and brought me further back into the "real world" after I had fallen so far. In many ways, as I am writing this, I think she may have been the turning point in my recovery and finding myself again. It started with her... and me, but then one day she introduced me at her house to two guys, Malcolm Brooks and John Nimock.

Rye, New York guys, kinda outta my social strata. But both real. We traded songs and stuff. John played piano and had a soft, beautiful voice, Malcolm at first glance had less skills, but on a silly argument over a harmony on "She'll be Comin Round the Mountain" (those who know me will tell you, I'm NEVER wrong on harmony, lol), but, well he was right. He couldn't really sing very well and I honestly don't remember the song that he wrote and sang. I just know it was better than anything I'd ever done. He has since, been in my life and has written so many amazing songs, I just don't remember which one this one was. But, I knew, in that moment, I was standing next to a real songwriter, which I, so far, wasn't. I was trying, but I just wasn't. I knew I needed Malcolm's help and I think he knew he could use my voice. Barbara and I shared a special moment in time and we parted as friends. She had no idea how she altered my path. Malcolm, John and I started to play together, adding a great tenor voice and friend of mine, Rick Bromfield, as our third voice, a guitar player and a friend of theirs named Russ Denooyer, a deep, thoughtful soul, who quit college at Brown, (I'm sure he was a hit at home for that), and just happened to be a great guitar player. Add a wonderful drummer, Barry Urich and we had a real band.

2/1/18... A step outside of the story... It was clearly starting to affect me, not so much in a good way, writing this, so I stopped. I think it's been 6 months or about that, but tonight, having dinner with someone who was proofing my work up to that date told me it was time to start again... Thanks Carol...

# DIANNE (AGAIN AND YET AGAIN)

Dianne... I've never written anything before in this format, other than a letter or college paper so I'm writing by memory only. Anyway, we have to back track a bit regarding Dianne and it remains one of the best stories of my tale. Before that last stretch of road, I was playing solo and one night at a small coffeehouse venue and a girl came up to me and said "My sister plays with your brother and said I had to come hear you'. I was pretty much full of myself (as I had finally had found the ground again, recovering from my personal fall, and which wouldn't change again until much later) I didn't think much about it at the time, or care. It was Dianne, and it was a brush of God and what would be the rest of my life even though I didn't know it at the time. Danny reminded me of an important moment that needs sharing though... He was playing with his partner Steve Preu and they were making their own way. One day Danny calls and says, "Hey we're rehearsing at (someone's house) and I should stop by", being the wonderful older brother... kidding, I did. They had about 10 musicians in the room with a fiddle, banjo, bass, electric guitar, mandolin... I mean every instrument you might need. They were rehearsing Billy Joel's "Travelin' Prayer", a piece way past most skill levels. The piece, although all the other instruments are necessary is centered around the piano. That player, that day was Dianne. Maybe nineteen or barely twenty. They started the song, (and I knew Steve and Danny wanted it to go well), and, all the players were great. When the solo came mid-song, I saw the best piano player. She quietly tore through a very… very hard piece of music. I watched with awe and admiration, cause it was great… well, just great. I left wondering who she was… but, again being Dave, I just went "Boy, she's good" and moved on. Lucky for me I got more than one chance.

She left my life and went back to college and her path back towards where she was thought she was headed. I continued on to where I was heading but in the long term stretch of life, she would be back pretty soon.

# THE MICHAEL BAND AND EARLY ADULTHOOD

However this early patch of road at this stage, became mostly about learning from Malcolm. He was truly a songwriter... And I wasn't... yet. But I could sing what he wrote. The reason we didn't climb all the way up the mountain, even though we were good enough was we had a community of egos... probably mostly mine. I sang Malcolm's songs, and mine and John and Rick, both great singers on their own, just got to sing just their songs... And Malcolm's songs were better than all of ours. I was totally good with it. I was singing the best work we had and I've been fairly clear that I was self-centered. Quickly, we rose up the local band ranks and were on a path towards NYC and bigger things.

We started drawing attention from players in the clubs and studios in the city. The most impressive was a fella named Ed Sprigg. He was an engineer at a world class studio called The Record Plant, I think he was a friend of Rick's but however it happened he heard some of our stuff and wanted to produce the band so he arranged for us to come in to the studio at off hours to record. At that time, John Lennon was working at the Record Plant, and Ed led us to believe he was friendly with him. He told us one night that John was at the studio so we should be aware just in case. He'd been on about this for awhile and no one took him too seriously. The complex had three studios, two on the first floor and one on, I think the thirteenth, which also had a game room where you could hang, with some video games and a pool table. That night, when we arrived, the girl at the front said, "Ed's coming down, stay here". He gets out of the elevator and says " We're working upstairs tonight". So... we get in and on the way up he says, "we'll need to wait a bit for the studio so let's go to the game room". No one thought anything about it... but... we get out of the elevator and headed towards it and Ed say's "be cool, John's in there". Now, at this moment in the story, I need to go back to the drive in we made that night. We had been discussing the "Lennon Factor" from Ed's story and Rush and the rest of the guys were praising the work of Mr. Lennon. I (again, being the fool that I clearly was, on a regular basis), said, "if I met McCartney, I'd be blown away, but Lennon, no... well, so, there we were at the door of the game room, me opening the door with the guys behind me... and... I walked in and looked to my right, and there was John Lennon with Harry Nillson (another known player on the national music scene), playing a video game. Well... I froze, and everybody bumped into me pushing us all into the room. No one else looked to the right so they remained unaware... I whispered, "there's John Lennon" and John Nimock, who must've thought I was kidding said, " yea right" then the rest of the guys saw him and I can't speak for anyone else but for an early twenty something kid, I was caught in a place I wasn't prepared for. I remember a pool table and a video game next to us. I turned to the game, as did John Nimock and said, "Wanna play" and he said , "sure", I said "gotta quarter", he said "no"... so we're standing there, just totally sure Lennon is looking at the clowns in the corner. Hoping to find anything to do, I see a water cooler with the cups on the side and figure, I'll get a cup of water, which I do, drink it and... here's the best part... as I've stated earlier in this story, I'm a pretty good athlete. The garbage can is one foot away from me... one foot, maybe less. I crumble the cup and throw it in the garbage can...

and, miss. Actually, missed by a lot. So… there is my cup, lying on the floor and I have to pick it up. My back is to Mister Lennon's and Harry Nillson and I'm certain they are watching this poor fool unraveling in front of God and them. I have no choice but to reach down, pick it up and drop it in the can. I do and slowly turn to face my fate. Lennon and his partner are deep into their game, laughing at something one had said to the other and oblivious to me or us or anything that just imploded in my world. We played some pool, hung out for awhile in the game room, actually calmed down a little and Ed came in and said, "studio's open". We got out of the room and Rush, who was always ready to help me out said, "So, Lennon wouldn't blow you away"… Point taken.

So… we recorded a record at The Record Plant and planned to enter the NYC scene. We had Warner Bros. interested and contacts with other major labels ready to come see what we had. Then John quit… and a few weeks later Rick quit too. I know why. I would try my best to talk them out of it but they were not getting the songs or time they deserved. I wish, now looking back that I could have seen their frustration, maybe Malcolm wishes it too, I don't know but we didn't so it came to pass. I don't need to spend much time on what happened next, although it took about two or three years out of our lives in what was a valiant but vain effort for Malcolm, Rush, Barry and I to carry on. And so now we come back to Dianne…

••••─────•─────••••

# DIANNE... (AGAIN )

S o... Dianne reappeared on the local music landscape during this time frame. But, before that, I need to go back and tell another rather important twist of all of our fates. Before John and Rick left the band and while we were still working at The Record Plant, as I have said we were gaining popularity in the Connecticut/ New York Music Scene. The most popular club at the time was a place called Gulliver's in Port Chester, just over the Connecticut border. It was a cover band spot, music every night, but we convinced them to let us play original music and so every Monday night we would fill the place. Every single Monday. I finally convinced the owners we were ready to play a weekend. They gave us one and we were so ready. But then Ed Sprigg calls us up and says "I've got the studio for Thursday, Friday and Saturday night, midnight to eight. We had to cancel the Gulliver's gigs. Needless to say they were not pleased. They got a regular cover band named Creation to fill in. That Friday night on our way into NYC about 11 we stopped at Gulliver's. Rush wanted cigarettes and I wanted to see the room. It was packed, and the band was good. Straight covers but good at what they did. I was pissed cause I wanted that weekend to prove we could hold the room with our own songs. Anyway, we headed into the city, and worked all night on our stuff, get home at eight in the morning and went to sleep til... I don't know, three or four in the afternoon. I wake up to the phone ringing and ringing... and ringing. I pick up the phone and it's my mother... "Oh my God!! you're alright!!" Let's remember, my mother was not the most effusive member of... well, any family. I said, "Yea, we were in the city last night, got home this morning and I just got up". She said" You said you were playing at Gulliver's this weekend!!". And I said "yea... but we got a chance to record so we cancelled". Then... she said "Gulliver's burned down last night. 24 people were killed in the fire". The world just sort of stopped. The band played down at the back and bottom of the room, and as I later learned, most of the band died in the fire and all the people closest to the music went with them. So... that's our missed bullet. Dianne... well, she, at the time was dating a prolific guitar player, and from what I've heard, a wonderful soul, Mark Thompson. As she tells her story, they were going thru a rough patch as most nineteen or twenty year olds do from time to time, but I think she truly loved him. Anyway, they were working their way back together and that Friday night he called her and said" Hey, were going down to Gulliver's to hear some music, come with us?... "As she tells her story, she was wavering on going but said, "No, but next time". Mark, who would've been right next to the band, being the musician that he was, died that night in the fire. I often think about our lives and the moments that alter the path. Is it chance... fate... God, or just blind circumstance? I honestly don't know and I don't think I ever will.

We played a Memorial Concert at an outdoor venue called the "Enzio Pinza Theater" that was both hard and gratifying. When you're young, I believe you will never truly appreciate how lucky or blessed you are. We moved on as if nothing had really happened.

Oh... did I mention Dianne started dating Rush?? Well... she did and became a member of the group of folks around the band and as the four of us tried our best to carry on, I was painfully aware that we had no chance. I did, however, know Dianne was a power in her own right and I also knew I needed her as the first piece of rebuilding the music. I had met a great, pretty girl named

Barbara Martella who became my real first serious partner. It was never gonna happen but it almost did. She wanted to get married and even though I never actually asked her, somehow I found myself looking at reception halls, churches… And oh… also, did I mention she had moved in to Dianne's apartment??? Well… being the coward that I am, I found, (it's too sad and long a story) it best to remove myself from our relationship. I'm not skipping it cause I don't want it here as part of the story, it's just that once you've been a part of a sadness that had no good story ending and the person you left behind in that story did nothing wrong it's hard to tell or probably to read. Barbara loved me and I did love her. Just not enough…

So, Rush wouldn't let his "girlfriend" in the band. That was some sort of band rule I guess… Ok, so one day he meets a girl at some gig and one thing leads to another, followed by a fight and an hour or so later I hear that they "broke up". To my credit, he did say to me that they broke up. I called Dianne and said " I hear you and Rush broke up? and she said "yea". I then said, "want to play in the band?" and she said yes before I finished the question. She knew rehearsals were at 9 every morning so I just said, "see you at rehearsal". "What about Rush?", she asked. Knowing where I was heading musically was possibly not yet in her mind but it was in mine. I just said, "I'll talk with him". It was not pleasant. Rush is brilliant, powerful and talented. But, I needed Dianne, so I pushed back harder and basically would not move forward without her. That, right there was the start of the demise of what was a very prolific, learning and passionate time of my life, but I was sure I had the beginnings of my next experience of consequence. That first day was hard. She was scared and Rush was, as I said, a strong presence… and really not happy about it at all. We were musically better immediately and everyone in the studio knew it. Malcolm, always a voice of calm and reason was first to say it out loud. Cut to the chase. The band lasted for a short time in this format (maybe one year, or a little more). I knew I was leaving and taking Dianne with me. A very hard day came in Dianne's apartment. I had spoken to her about us moving on and she was on board but remained unsure of the change, knowing that the rest of us had been together for so long. One of those moments. Rush was in total denial… Malcolm just tried his best to help probably his closes and oldest friend… He said, "Rush, they don't need us anymore". That moment broke my heart. I had learned more from Malcolm and took something with me from Rush, about writing (Malcolm) and playing (Rush) and playing inside a "band", but it was time to go on in one of the top ten hardest days of my life.

# PART ONE

**NOTE:** As I am writing this story I need to pause to reflect. It's July 2018 right now… today. This part of not just my life, but the lives of so many others who have shared in the experience surrounding the next turn of events reflect how amazingly it can all just turn on a dime. My life, Dianne's and all the folks who I will be storytelling about in the upcoming pages and then eventually my two very special daughters (each in their own unique way) are all tied to this island by a simple twist of fate. I'm not sure how this will all unfold on paper so I'll call this Part One. It surely can't all be told in a simple section because next month will mark the 45th year of our time on the island, (August 1978) so I'll see how it goes… as it goes, inside the rest of the story. See you often just go… up the road we came on…

# STORY #27

## UP THE ROAD

Playing with Dianne quickly changed the dynamic of the band and how I saw us proceeding. Another great voice and her piano playing started to make me start to believe again. Add to that a life altering direction change and you have an interesting summer on your hands. I didn't mention Dianne had finished college, got the prime job in our town at the high school teaching music and was, as a life path goes, on her way... but... we were playing a club in Westport called The Player's Tavern, it was a pretty cool venue cause it was part of a complex that also housed The Westport Playhouse, an out of the city but "in" theater. Paul Newman, Joanne Woodward sponsored it and anyone who wanted to slip out of NYC and try new works would find a home at the Playhouse. So, one night we're playing at the Tavern and a young girl comes up in a break and says, "You guys are great! My Mom books a club in St. Croix and you'd be perfect!!" At the time I had no idea where St. Croix was, but it sounded like something I might do. The band had been full time committed to music for so long... But... Dianne had a REAL JOB. And I don't say that lightly. Plus, I knew her family... Her Dad. This wasn't going to go well. For her... I presented the option to the band and I'm not sure, as to when Di would "come to her senses" and opt out. She never blinked... "I'm in", and I remember saying, "Your father's not going to like this", and let's remember, she was all of 22 at the time. She again said, "I'm in", I doubt I would have gone without her. I don't think I ever said that out loud, or even thought about it till right now. If she had said no, I might have turned it down and stayed. But she didn't, so I guess I'll never know. So we were going to St. Croix.

•••◆•—————◆—————•◆•••

# ANXIETY: SOMEONE WHO I LIVED WITH... STARTING BACK THEN TILL NOW

My tale takes a turn here. One I never thought it would. But I guess no story is without it's share of darker, rockier roads. I won't stay long on this cause it's no fun to write and I'll bet not to read either.

I never really hurt anyone up to this point. I mean, really hurt, did something bad and got caught. I mentioned my girlfriend Barbara a number of pages back... and we were coming to a close of our relationship. One night we got into a fight, and I left, went to a bar we played at often... and... the rest went off the rails. A week or two before we left for the island I was with someone else. Barbara was hurt... bad, and I had never done that to someone or seen THAT look in their eyes. I still cannot forget it. So, a few days later I was in the Colony Grill and suddenly I couldn't breathe. The bartender, Fitz, who I'd known all my life, brought me my pie (pizza), put it down, looked at me and said "Davey, you ok?". I put some money down and ran... just to get outside... I had never been in this kind of real trouble psychologically before... but I sensed that I was now. It happened again later that day... And then, again, and, again. I had no idea what an anxiety attack was, hell, up to here in my life, I didn't know what anxiety was... but I was about to learn. Plus, I was going on a three month trip... So, we go and I arrived in the Caribbean... first time I had been in the region and the beauty was and is still beyond words. I convinced myself I would be fine. But, in spite of my surroundings, I was at the beginning of living with what would be a lifelong pal or enemy and who would dog me right up till this day. I have learned to live with the dog. I don't have to like it, but we share the same space and eventually I found a way to cope with it so I will leave it here because it doesn't deserve any more space or time in this tale, just to say, from my heart, to anyone who suffers from anxiety, depression or any other thing that drags you down, a mental enemy... As I have said before in this story my Dad used to say "if you don't quit... they can't beat you". I believe that and it has pulled me through many, many bad moments, and if you have been brushed by it in any way, I think you need to believe it too. So, now back to a real change in the weather...

# THE STRAND, FREDRIKSTED, AUGUST 1978

We landed on St. Croix not knowing what to expect. We were met by one of the owners of the club we were playing at. It was called The Strand. His name was Beek and he had an old truck to carry our equipment back to where we would be calling home for the next three months. Mid-island, which is where the airport is, did not do the island justice. The actual colors of the Caribbean were already making their presence known but it was clouded, mostly by old streets, small shacks and poor conditions for all who lived there. But as we drove and got closer to the coast, the colors did start to take control. The Strand was on a street at the edge of the water and it took my breath away. We unloaded the equipment from the truck, but it was August in the Caribbean and hot really didn't really do it justice, it was HOT... still, we were excited and young, so on we went. We were playing on the second floor of this old Danish building that looked like it had been there since the 1700s, (it, in fact, had). We had rooms down the hall from the club, The Strand was a hotel (loose term), restaurant, (also super loose term) and mostly a bar/club. The club was above a jewelry store (Little Switzerland) and we learned part of the band's job every night was after they closed the store we would put eight metal posts up from floor to ceiling inside below us and take them down after the gig. When we asked why, the bartender smiled and said "so the building doesn't collapse"... This was a high tech operation... We had been in town all day and Frederiksted was and still is, what I would describe as an 1830's two story Old West town out of a dime novel, dropped down on a Caribbean island with a black Cruzan culture filling in for your American Wild West B movie cast. The first day I met maybe five Americans from the states, all at the club. I didn't think the poles downstairs were gonna be necessary unless we had a real popular Cruzan crowd... The rooms we would be living in can only be described as, well, bad... I mean by St. Croix standards, which we, at the time were totally unaware of, they weren't that bad. But by all we knew... rattling air conditioners, (when they worked), beds, well, sort of beds, and bugs... and I'm not talking American bugs... I'm talking BIG bugs... that fly... at you.. I wasn't happy and I'm pretty sure Dianne was really not happy, although to her credit I never heard her complain. So, we settled in to our new reality in a hurry cause we were playing that night. Never will forget that night. I have played a lot of places and venues in my life. Some pretty big and many just regular bar band gigs. Nothing prepared me for that first night on St. Croix... The deal we had was six nights a week, Tuesday thru Sunday, 10 to 2, which, at that time of our lives were pretty standard hours. Around nine o'clock, from my room, I heard what sounded like a loud crowd down the hall towards the bar. I walked out and looked into the room and saw that it was jammed! A totally integrated group of people and already at a state of party, ready I had rarely seen before in my life... The Americans were a combination of young cowboy/cowgirl like locals, as I was to learn over the next months, some who became lifelong friends and all of whom were way crazier than I was (which I thought at the time was saying something), Some tourists, believe me, they stood out, local Cruzans and an assortment of various down island folks. I went back and told the band this was gonna be a new experience. That would prove to be a forty five year understatement which I am still living and experiencing to this day. It was probably 100 degrees in the club with wall to wall people as we walked in to play. From our first note til our last chord at 2 a.m. they danced… I was sure the eight poles down below us weren't enough and still to this day don't believe the building didn't come down. And it wasn't just dancing… it was… dancing with total abandon. The night was like no night of music I can remember. I came to learn over these many years that the type of person living on an outward Caribbean island in the late 70s was cut from, as I said before "crazier than I am" cloth. I saw myself as a step off the main road but these folks were not just off the road, they were deep in the woods and happy to remain there. I have come to love it and them deeply, but during those first days it was way past intimidating. Every stateside American living on the west end of the island (and there were maybe only 50 or 60 of them) were seemingly afraid of no one or anything in their paths. They lived in a Cruzan town, where they were not welcome, by a society that had lived there for centuries, and did not want them in their town, but as I learned they chose to carve out their place on the island and fought fiercely for that right. Every man and woman carried themselves in a way I can only describe as fearless. It was a dangerous time with a lot of racial tension. Had we known prior to going, things might have been very different, if I had known, I and many folks that came down with me over the years would have missed a life changing opportunity. But… on that night it was a thrilling moment. I met folks over the course of this first trip that changed the way I saw how we all deal with our individual situations, hopes, dreams and realities. Many of the upcoming stories will introduce you to some of those wonderful souls…

# CHEECH: MY FIRST BIG BROTHER

The first guy that I remember changing my life since Artie Evanchek was Willie Thomas, aka Cheech on St. Croix. He was, in my eyes, the unofficial leader of the local American community in Frederiksted. He lived up in the Rain Forest in a geodesic dome above a mahogany woodshop named Leap. I know that sounds… a little strange. In the first days on St. Croix, believe me, nothing was not strange, everything was strange. I was used to being in control of my life and I felt it was my responsibility to be sure of the situation I put my bandmates in. Well, that game plan was clearly out the door. After our first night, the high of the intensity and passion of the local folks wore slightly away and we began to adjust to being the "the new kids" in F'sted and started finding our daily way in this new environment. It started at a place called "Rainbow Beach", a local, on the beach bar, that seemed to be the main spot for the place to spend our daytimes. Most of the kids we met at the club said "Rainbow" when we asked what or where… so on we went. We were the band so that went a long way towards getting us in with the local community and it really did feel good. So, there we are, on this amazing beach, after a more amazing night and I'm starting to feel like this was gonna be good. Well, in walks Cheech… I can only describe him as a cross between Tarzan and some rock star. He was cut, good looking, confidently arrogant and everybody in the bar took it for granted.

Let me say, after such a description, he may sound in some way less then I wish him to be portrayed, he was a real good guy. His eyes scanned the bar and the beach, he landed on me, walked over and said, "Hey Man, saw you guy's last night at the bar, I had a real good time". Had no idea how to answer that... were we good, or were we just there and he had a good time... Trying my best to remain on level ground I said, "We had a pretty good time too, didn't know what to expect but it was real good fun". He smiled and said, "I'm Willie, but everybody calls me Cheech... you need anything just let me know, ok?. It was clear from that moment right up till today that Willie felt he was capable of whatever he said he could and or would do. The story now becomes more about the people who followed him when we first met on the island... I became a passenger on their trail... the first and really good story follows...

## BIG JAKE, CHEECH AND ME

First week, Frederiksted, trying to hang with the local gang… On this particular day, Cheech introduced me to Big Jake… he was an ex-NFL lineman who had both shoulders busted up to a point where it put him out of the league, and I met him on that day, down island now and crossing paths. Anyway, Jake was a big guy, maybe 6'5" or so, 250 pounds and we were at a bar called "Beulahs". It was a room about 15 by 15 and she served just one drink, "Beulah's Fantails". She told no one what was in it, it was Rum, some fruit punch… but, was rumored to have a "special something" in the drink which made it different. According to the locals, one Fantail was okay, but two was treading on shaky ground. As I learned later, it was an herb she grew up in the rain forest, which contained something comparable to Belladonna, or Mescaline. Well, we were on our second, (middle of the afternoon) and I was starting to enjoy these two very different men. a lot… Till… well, in walked seven men, Latin, I found out later, Puerto Rican, and they were focused on Jake. He turned, slowly towards these men and one of them said, "we're here to make you pay for what you did to my sister". Jake, then surmised the woman they were talking about was someone he had seen, dated and, as often happens, (especially, as I was also to learn later, referring to relationships on the island) Jake had moved on. Right around then, Beulah, with a really big Cruzan accent started yelling at…

well, everyone. What she was saying, I have no idea. I had been
on island for about five or six days, and couldn't understand one
word. It was English, but nothing I could take in. Jake and Cheech
however, knew just what she was saying and Jake, calmly, and
with a slow, deliberate reply to both her and the men facing us
said, "OK, you guys want me dead, but let's not bust up Beulah's
place. Go outside and we'll (we'll??) be out in a minute". These
fella's facing us clearly didn't know what to do, but Beulah started
yelling again and me, being the only one in the room who couldn't
understand what she was saying, was way out of my element.
But... the Puerto Rican brother, glaring, but obviously unsure
of what to do said, "there's no other way out of here!". Jake kind
of waved his hand and said, "we'll be right out". They walked
out into the street and it was suddenly very quiet in the room...
Jake, (who I had met about an hour before, turns to Cheech, who
I've known for four or five days, looks at him and says, "can he
fight? So, Cheech turns to me, with this "moment in a movie"
look and says, "I don't know, can you fight?". Well, I have, as has
been written in this story, been in quite a few, but this felt a little
different. Anyway, not to appear weak, scared or less of a tougher
guy than these two, I said, "yea, I can fight". So Jake says, "OK,
when we go out, you pick the biggest guy and you take him.". I
countered with, "uh, there are seven guys out there". "Yea", he
kinda drawls, "you get him". I said, "and you two take the other
six?". No kidding, I mean really, Cheech says, "they're small"...
Okay, now I'm so, again, unsure of my ground, I got nothin', so I
just (keeping in mind we were well on onto our second "Fantail")
stood up and walked out first into the street. Pretty sure I surprised
the boys, but I looked back and they were right there.

Now, I pause to set a scene, I will never forget as long as I
live. On Strand Street in F'sted, stood seven men from one side
of the street to the other. This was a real time, real life, uh-oh,
movie moment. I looked across at Jake and Cheech and they're
both sort of smilin'... I, on the other hand... am not. My Dad,

who as I have already said taught me how to fight as a child in our basement had said, "Get the first punch in" so I pointed at the biggest guy in the group and started at him. I saw surprise in his eyes but I was more interested in the first punch. Which I got. He was almost my size and fast he glanced it off and hit me pretty good, but my next punch caught him square in the jaw and he went down… couldn't have been more than 15 or 20 seconds. I got ready to jump on him when he got up and ran… I had no idea why. I turned around and saw Jake and Cheech looking like Ninja warriors with six guys on the ground, all hurt bad enough to not be moving very well. I could not fathom what had happened but they both quietly walked back into Beulah's and I followed. We sat down and Jake said "Good Job", Cheech laughed and said "I told you he could fight" and winked. I said "who the hell are you guys??" It is one of most lasting memories of my life.

# AND THEN IT GOT WORSE

So, we started playing every night (Tuesday- Sunday) at the club and it was August, beyond hot, and every night the club was jammed full. I have already touched on this before but to say I had no idea where these people were coming from was interesting but I didn't care, it was a blast. We saw the same 30-40 white kids every day on the streets and beaches but not all these people. There was a thermometer on the wall and every night it hit 110 degrees We had rooms down the hall and changed clothes after every set. But the vibe was without question as exciting a venue as I have ever experienced. However after the fight, word started to spread that the Latin/Cruzan community in F'sted was growing darker and fueled with more anger about the "white young people" not belonging. As a band, we were not part of this battle, but just by being there we were. We were there and it was happening. The next day, a local American businessman was killed in his home out West where we were and it made the front pages of The New York Times. Dianne's father called (let's remember I'm not his favorite guy around this time) and got me on the phone at The Strand and told me to 'send my daughter home now." Not being her boyfriend and at the time just a bandmate, I suggested he talk to her. (More big points for me later in life). She stayed, but the talk on the street that there was going to be something that weekend at the club between the two groups of people. This not being our fight, and feeling responsible for getting us in this, I found a way to the roof of the building, and over to the next street where if it went bad we were gonna go and I told everyone to be prepared for that if this got as dangerous as it looked and was appearing to be. We started every night at 10 and by 9 o'clock there were 50 or 60 of the local kids inside the Strand. The bad news was there were two or three hundred Cruzan's outside making noise, carrying torches and this was heading in what appeared to be more than I'd ever seen in the way of a battle.

There was a guy who I only knew as "Mole". A short bull of a guy who had a weapon in clear sight. In fact there were at least 30 weapons in clear sight. I was about to take us out the way we talked about when I heard Mole say "Aw, Fuck this!" the club where we played was on the second floor with windows opening to the street/park by the ocean below. Mole walked to the window and fired shots above the crowd. I swear you couldn't (at least I couldn't) hear anything. He yelled out "We don't want this fight! If there's trouble many people will die! We just want to live here in peace! Go home, take your children home! This should not happen!!!… Silence… Cheech walked up behind me and said "Why don't you guys play something soft , maybe we can calm this down". I picked a song Malcolm wrote called "House of Stone" and we started. I didn't see it myself but I was told that slowly the crowd began to disperse and within a few songs most were gone. The tension of the night stayed but there was no trouble, and in the days that followed it felt like a dam had broken and the anger had somehow lessened. But I believe that was as close to this level of danger as I ever had or have seen since.

••◦•———————————◦———————————•◦••

# A DOWN ISLAND STORY OF DUMB, FEAR AND THEN PURE JOY

A last F'sted story. As I said we stayed on the island for long stretches of time. I was in love with a Cuban girl named Rosie Garcia and saw no reason to go home whether we were playing or not One of the owners of the Strand was Jerry Press. As I have said all the Americans on the West End of the island were strong, courageous and really a little bit crazy. On this particular day Jerry asked me if I was interested in making $500 dollars by helping him on a sail down island. I said I had no knowledge of boats or sailing and he replied "I just need another body and I can show you what I would need you to do." $500 dollars in the 70's was a lot of money and I trusted Jerry a lot so I said I would go. He explained we would safely sail down the chain of islands so we were almost always within sight of land. We were going to St. Lucia where he had to pick up some cargo to bring back to St. Croix. Let me say I had no idea what "cargo" meant, I think I realized later but naïve is a word that would describe me at that time in my life. So we left from the East End of the Island in a 38 foot sailboat and started on the journey, First St. Martin, then through many smaller islands then to Dominica, Martinique and eventually arriving on St. Lucia. He met with another gentleman and then his men loaded many boxes onto the bottom of the boat.

I saw an exchange of money (lots of money), again me, naïve. That night Jerry paid me and took me out to a local restaurant that was amazing. However, during the dinner he said, "It took us longer to get here than I thought because we were sailing against the tradewinds so I think we need to go straight across the Caribbean Sea to make up the time". This sounded like a very bad idea to me and I asked if it wasn't safer to go back the way we had come and he said he have a deadline to be back on St. Croix to make this delivery so I (not we) were going to have to make up the time with a more direct route. He then said "we'll leave at first light" and I guessed that the discussion was over. He seemed confident so I sort of let it go which looking back now was probably a terrible idea but... So, we leave St. Lucia at daybreak and head directly out into open ocean. He said that the boat was seaworthy and it would be no problem and my experience, being none, believed him. He thought it would take only 5 or 6 days so we brought food for the trip. It had taken us two and a half weeks to get to St. Lucia. On this one fact he was wrong. After 6 days we still had no sight of land and the food was almost gone. All that we had left then was water, vodka and, don't ask me why, butter. This was starting to become alarming to me so I asked how he knew where he was going and said "the North Star". Well, that didn't seem like the best navigational piece of equipment so my concern began to grow. Day seven came and went and on day eight we had no food left and still no sight of land. He explained how the wind, which was supposedly in our favor had died so we were not moving as fast as he had hoped. And then again, there is the sun. In the island chain the land forms clouds but in an open sea there is no land, so just sun. We are sailing through that day when at first I thought I was hallucinating or imagining it. I said to Jerry "Is that a palm tree?? He looked out and said "Hot Damn!!" and turned the boat towards it. Within 20 minutes or so it became clear that there was a tiny piece of land, almost really not even an island. As we pulled up Jerry was laughing and either losing it or was just plain giddy.

We dropped anchor in about 15-20 feet of water. He smiles and looks at me and says "I'll be right back!" and then dives off the boat towards the bottom. Now, let's remember, Jerry is a big man pushing 280-300 pounds. I can see him clearly on the bottom but not moving at all. I'm starting to panic cause if he's had a heart attack or any other reason to be dead well than so was I. I can't sail a boat!! It felt like 5 minutes but was probably a minute or maybe a little more when I see Jerry reach out right and then reach back left and swim up towards the surface! He came out of the water in what I can only describe as a whale breaking out of the ocean and threw two HUGE lobsters onto the boat. The bigger one was at least probably 8 pounds and the little one was maybe 6!! He climbs up the rope ladder and smiles and says "Dinner!!!" On our propane grill was a metal pot full of water waiting to boil and we could only get one lobster in at a time and even then it was still was tight. So, as Jerry smiled at me and said, "I told you we might need butter!". We ate as much lobster as we could, only time in my life that I can say that and drank vodka. Jerry said, "If this piece of land is here than we're close", I asked why and quite logically he told me that this small piece of land means we're close to other lands in the chain. We went to sleep that night mildly drunk (lol) and for the first time since we set out from St. Lucia I had the feeling this might work out. In the morning, both of us hungover, we left our oasis and continued on. Well, within about 3 or 4 hours I said "Jerry!!! there's land!!!" He smiled and said nothing. We were heading directly towards safety. Now, as I realize afterward, St. Croix is the only island in the entire Antilles chain that sits inside the Caribbean Sea. As we get closer Jerry says, "that's St.Croix". I thought no way, but as we got closer even I saw this was the East End of the island as we headed towards Point Udall at the eastern most land on the island. We came around towards a mooring in what was loosely called St. Croix Yacht Club. I said "my God, you did it!", and he smiled and said, "you gotta get lost I've got some business to attend to". He gave me another hundred dollars and said, "nice job now go"… Which I did. I saw him that night back in F'sted on the other side of the island at the Strand and he bought me a drink and said, "just to be clear, that never happened". It was one of the few times in my life, I had absolutely… no words…

···•━━━•━━━•━━━•···

# CHRISTIANSTED (PHASE 1)

So a normal day over the next three months while playing any gig was from 10-2 hanging out awhile, going to bed, getting up around noon and walking down to place I referred to earlier called Rainbow Beach. It was the local favorite spot about a mile out of town and since we had no car our options were limited. But it was still great. Got to know the local American West-enders and fell into a slow paced daily routine. I still couldn't figure where all the people every night at the gigs were coming from. I mean we were packed every night! So we're about 2 ½ months into the trip, and one of the owners of the club (Bruce) asked me if I wanted to ride into town to pick up some supplies. I figured we were going to some local store but as we were driving we kept getting further and further from town I asked "Where are we going?" He said "Christiansted" to which as having been as sheltered inside our daily west end routine I said "There's another town on this island??" He laughed and said something like "You guys really don't get around much do you?" Let's try to explain the next hour. First, Frederiksted looks much the same as it did in the late 1700s with old stone Danish architecture and many buildings which have just fallen into decay over the years. On any given day you might see 10-20 people going about their daily business. I remember turning the corner at the top of the hill and driving down the main street of Christiansted towards the center of town. We passed an old church which looked to be 300 years old, a magnificent old piece of history from another time. But, looking down the street I saw HUNDREDS of people and the buildings, though representative of F'sted with the same Danish design they were all immaculate and it looked like I was seeing my first color TV program! Brilliant yellow, blues and every other color you can imagine, each building it's own piece of artwork. Shops, restaurant's and music venues everywhere.

I'll take a moment here to describe the state of the band and our fairly soon departure from The Strand and St. Croix. Everyone had found someone they cared for and I don't think anyone wanted to leave. I saw what looked like a big venue in the very center of town called Pearl's. I asked Bruce if I could jump out and look around and he said sure he'd be back in a while. I walked up two hundred year old steps and into a big room with a full band set up at the end. A guy was sitting at the bar alone (it was before noon) and I asked him who books the bands? He said "I do, why you got a band?' with a slight smile. I said "Yea, we're playing out west at the Strand", and he turned to me and said "I've heard about you guys, were you there during the trouble?" I said we were but we're going back to the states in a few weeks and nobody wants to go". I introduced myself and his name was Peter de Chardin, who would become a lifelong friend to me. Anyway he said he'd come and check us out. Well, he did, I guess he liked what we heard and booked us for 3 more months, but this time we were in TOWN.

‣‣◆▬━━━━◆━━━━▬◆‣‣

# CHRISTIANSTED (PHASE 2)

So needless to say, the band was all in and we got on an old
flatbed truck and hauled all our stuff across the island. Where
Frederiksted was "West", Christiansted was "East". We went from
a quiet laid back lifestyle to a thriving fast moving daily existence.
They were building rooms above the club for the bands to live in
that were far from finished, but everybody had four walls, a door
and a bed. We nicknamed it the "Plywood Palace", cause, well, it
was. Walls were plywood and they each had, basically a cot and a
small drawer with one bathroom to share. Dianne was a trooper
back then and managed to put up with "the boys". Similar to our
daily routine in F'sted, get up go to the beach, go back to the club
and play, life was much the same in Christiansted. We found a
beach on a small island out in the harbor. It had a hotel and was
appropriately named "Hotel on the Cay". It was a one minute
ferry ride over and was amazing! This small island was inside the
reef protecting the harbor so the water was like glass, whereas in
Frederksted at Rainbow we were in open ocean where waves and
currents could be challenging. The difference was extreme and
much to everyone's taste. Little did I know then that I would be
on this beach almost daily over 45 years later (yikes!). But back
to the new club. Pearl's had a much bigger stage and was a larger
room. Our first night playing the room was full an hour before we
even started, with a line out the door. I was feeling pretty special

till the bartender said "Yea, there's three stateside bands playing in town and they're all in the same boat... ... So much for Mr. Popularity. However this started some of the most fun I ever had playing on a daily basis. The band was really good and every night the people would literally shake the building! And every night had a different story. Way too many to tell now, but it reminded me of the movie "Animal House" (only night after night). So, our Tuesday to Sunday life proceeded for the next three months till it was time to go but since nobody wanted to leave we moved down the street to a place called the "Grandstand Play". Dianne and I and Danny (next story) were at the time negotiating a record deal with RCA and we had a backer who saw us through his daughter Donna and was a Greenwich businessman named Pete Frankel with the funds to help us along the way. We should have been back in NYC months before but... anyway he got us a gig at The Bitter End in Greenwich Village , which was at the time(actually it still is) was the spot to play for showcasing your songs to a New York crowd always full of people from the New York record scene. So we fly home for two days to do the gig and fulfill Mr. Frankel's faith in us and that we still wanted a future on the recording landscape. Well, the gig went great and we went back to St. Croix the next day. A few days pass and he calls and said RCA wants to do an album, a one record deal. The good news was they had no studio room for about two months so we got to stay on the island and fulfill our agreement with the Grandstand. Of the three stateside band clubs Grandstand was recognized as "the" spot so it worked out and that was to become our main place on the island for a number of years to follow.

# DANNY

We had been playing as a duo up here much of the time prior to St. Croix and started working with my brother Danny. I have spoken about him in many stories here prior to this. Earlier that year, as I have already wrote about, I had gone to hear Danny play with his band at an outdoor concert and remember thinking how talented he was… and slowly he began to add the missing part and quickly it became obvious that he was going to be the third singer in the band and also we began writing as a team. We played almost every night in Connecticut and NYC and finally came to take the music industry seriously. I honestly think though that the first years in STX, being, as I said, the most exciting, did a lot of harm to our attempt at reaching the next level. So, we were now a trio primarily. We would add members to fit the venue if it called for it, but Sister Sun was Danny, Dianne and me.

# STORY #37

❰•◦••━━━•━━━•━━━••◦•❱

# RCA

This was a very strange time for the three of us. RCA was getting ready to start a rehearsal schedule but we were playing with New York studio musicians who, while amazingly talented, didn't, I believe, understand the type of music we were trying to produce. I lobbied hard for us to do the record ourselves and Ethel Gabriel, a Vice President of the RCA Record Division, reluctantly said ok. My mistake #1. We had little experience in a major studio and no chemistry with the new guys in the band. The only one we had ever played with a a drummer named Perry Cavari (who went on to be a major Broadway player). Early on he said to me" I don't feel this group of people are all on the same page". He was right and what became a decent album was only that. A decent album. At the time there were two studios on the ground floor, Studios A & B and gym like huge Studio on the 10th floor for large project involving an entire orchestra. Studio C. I tell you this because while we were doing our project in Studio A, another duo was starting their first record in Studio B. Their names were Lindsey and Stevie. We became friendly in the lounge that connected the two rooms and spent some time together. Their album was recorded by a career RCA producer. When both albums were completed we were asked to see Ms. Gabriel in her office. She simply said I can only release one of these records and I'd like you to help me with it. She played a song of ours which was one of the better songs and then she played a song of theirs. As songs go, we were comparable, but theirs sounded like a "record" while ours sounded smaller and far less polished. She had made her point and it was obvious. "I should never have let you produce your own record. Your songs are as good or better than theirs but they sound well recorded and yours, like badly produced work". Needless to say, we were pretty beaten down but she was right. What happened next was to become a real unique part (probably in a very bad way)of our story and our careers. She said, "I know a producer in London who is very popular in Europe named Henry Hadaway and I want you to go to England and try this again. Could have knocked us over with a feather.

---

# LONDON

We began this part of the journey with high expectations. We were staying at a small hotel directly across from Hyde Park. We met Henry Hadaway the next day and he seemed eager to get the best musicians in London to join us in his studio and get to work. This sounded exciting and we found ourselves in the London nightlife scene at the highest levels. I struck up a unique relationship with a man named Kenny Lynch, who could be compared to Johnny Carson here in America. He had a similar late night show on the BBC and was extremely popular. While I spent time with him in public he was constantly stopped for autographs or pictures. I just liked him and I guess he liked me but to me it started as him being just Kenny. We found ourselves at numerous parties that just dripped of a "who's who" quality, but we had not begun work on the album. Finally I asked Henry when he thought we'd be starting the project. His next comment was rattling. He said "my producer is almost done with the arrangements". We had not heard one note of music and I (we) became wary of what type of sound they were envisioning for us. And, as we started, the direction that they were taking was not anything close to how we saw our music. Needless to say as the summer unfolded it became apparent we were again not on the same page with our producer so it became a long summer.

During this time the IRA and England were locked in a war over the freedom of Ireland remaining part of the British Empire. It's been ongoing since the early 1900's and during our time there it had escalated dramatically. Danny and I were jogging/walking in Hyde Park one morning and suddenly an explosion rocked the whole city. I said "that was a bomb". The IRA had detonated an enormous bomb outside of Buckingham Palace where the Royal Guard were on horseback, killing most of the men and horses. Suddenly sirens from all over the city made it clear something terrible had happened. We ran back to our rooms and saw what had occurred on television. We were very close to a hospital and almost immediately ambulances began roaring past us. This was really the first time any of us had seen this type of violence up close involving people and government. Right then a second explosion, much closer to us literally rocked the building. We were near the place where an outdoor concert by the Royal Band (I'm still not sure of what their actual title was) but the IRA had placed a second bomb under the bandstand in which we later learned was called "Regents Park", again killing most if not all of the musicians and injuring many in the crowd. Had we had known about the concert I'm almost sure we would have been there. Many more ambulances drove by and all of London became quiet. But there was no doubt it was also a war zone under attack. News continued throughout the day and fear of more attacks remained at the forefront of every television in the city. The day passed without further event but the tension was almost palpable. Just to do something we went to a nearby theater, where believe it or not the movie "Rocky" was playing. As we went to buy our tickets a policeman asked our nationalities. Being mostly Irish I went with "American" but it really spooked me. Halfway thru the movie something literally hit the building and it was close to a panic situation. The lights went up and a police officer came forward and told the audience that a car had hit the theater and nothing more. Almost no one stayed for the rest of the movie. I think everyone had had more than enough for one day.

To basically wrap up our summer in England, our record was terrible, our spirits were way down and our hope of a recording contract looked very dim. We returned to America and started right back where we left off, playing the clubs in Connecticut and New York, and then going back to St. Croix which had almost become a second home.

●●◆●●━━━━●━━━━●●◆●●

# BILLY/CONNECTICUT AND FREDERICKSTED

There was no specific time to bring my friend Bill SanFanAndre into my story. I met him one night 45 some odd years ago in Darien, Connecticut. I went to a party with my girlfriend Barbara who also lived on Darien and I didn't know a soul in the room although she seemed pretty popular. But there was one guy who stood out as clearly as the center of the event. I asked Barbara who he was and she said "That's Billy, he's pretty much the leader of this bunch. So I stayed on the sidelines most of the night and a bunch of guys were all playing ping pong and Bill was beating them one after another, and they were all very good. I played a ton of Ping Pong at Fordham cause I played on the tennis team and all winter it was all we did, and I had the advantage of watching him play six or seven games and you can learn a lot about any player by watching. When the last one seemed done I walked up to Bill and said "Hi, I'm Dave, I came with Barbara" He had a big smile which in later years I would learn that smile so well. I said "You up for one more game?". He grinned and said "Sure". We played three games in a row. The first one, he wasn't taking me seriously until it was too late and he lost. We had gotten most of the party's attention and he smiled again and said "One more?", I said sure. A Ping Pong game goes to 21 but you have to win by two (23-21 or 25-23, much like a tiebreaker in tennis). We were tied at 21 and the game continued. Billy won, I think it was 29-27. By now this was the party... So I said "two out of three?" and he said "couldn't be any other way'… it again went to a tiebreaker, but this time I got away with a 24-22 win. He came around the table, we shook hands and he asked me my name. I told him , he told me his and I said "this is pretty much your room". He laughed and said "It's my parent's house!". I said okay but that's not what I meant and he smiled and replied, "I know but thanks, they're all good friends". He invited me back and as I got into the car with Barbara I said to her "that's gonna be my best friend", and for the next twenty years he was just that. He was in my Wedding, I was in his, and we were inseparable for a very long time. There's a lot more to tell but I'm gonna pause here to decide if I want to because although so much of it was the best time of my life.

# SECOND STORY

One more great story which truly capture Billy humor and spirit. He was a Connecticut, Darien boy, who never wanted for anything in his whole life. I missed that trip. But as our friendship grew I became part of his life and he became part of mine. His family was wealthy, and he was taught only what he knew. We lived together sharing various houses with Danny and many others. He taught me golf, (one of the only sports I had never played, and he was the State High School Champ), and I introduced him to the world of music. He was an amazing golfer and I wasn't. I got better as time went on but never reached his level and I'm okay with that... My second story starts here...

So for Billy St. Croix was a world away in too many ways. I had been in St. Croix many times for that first a couple of years and Cheech asked me if I could watch the dome for a month because he was traveling with Jerry Press (I've already spoke of and one of the three owners of the Strand), and I have no idea what they might have been doing... that's my story and I'm sticking with it... anyway. also to explain the term "dome", Cheech lived in a geodesic dome (I believed it was Buckminster Fuller who originally designed them) and there he was. As I have said he lived above a workshop called "Leap" with made amazing artwork out of mahogany wood which was plentiful on the island. So Billy decided to come down, unaware as any one might possibly be and we stayed at the Dome and we had Cheech's truck to get around in. He truly had no idea the world he was actually walking into. But as time went on Billy got more and more relaxed living in this semi-wild west town. So Cheech gets back having accomplished whatever it was they were doing, and Billy and I had about a week left before heading back to states. Billy was always a big happy drinker and in the Strand one night he was hanging with this local girl when Cheech said we had to get home. I went and Bill who also needed to go, but didn't as he was well on his happy drinker way and said he'd stay and the young lady would give him a ride home. I asked if she had a four wheel drive vehicle and she didn't. Now, to understand where the dome is, it's at the top of a very steep climb in the middle of the Rain Forest and the road up the hill was not doable without a four wheel car or truck. Add that to the fact, that if you're ever in the Rain Forest at night you can't see your hand in front of your face. I told Bill this was a real bad idea, but he was not about to leave, Cheech sort of smiled and said "OK bud, we'll see you at home". We both knew he was now in way over his head. Cheech said, "We all gotta learn sometime" so home we went. I said he could die out here and Cheech promised we'd go get him when the lesson was learned. At night out West you can almost feel the silence. We were at the Dome having a beer when we heard a car leaving Fredericksted and turning onto Mahogany Road which went thru the Rain Forest. Cheech said "that'll be our boy". Heard him get out of the car the bottom of the hill, laughing and saying goodbye to his lady friend. Now at the start of the road up, there's a small bridge where the runoff from the rain on the mountains flows under it. The car left and we waited. About five or ten seconds go by and we hear the first splash of somebody going into the water off the bridge. "Shit!!"and Cheech smiled and said "ready?". I didn't know what he meant til I heard the second splash. Billy, it seems had walked off one side of the bridge climbed back up and walked right off the other. I said "C'mon Cheech and he said "Oh no, not yet"… now we didn't hear another sound for a long time. At this point I need to give Billy a sincere compliment. Here's a preppy Darien guy completely out of his element two thousand miles from anything he's ever known. Now on the side of the road up to the Dome there was a huge rut, almost a ditch. Cheech had been clear to us before he left if you hit the rut the truck will not go any farther. As Billy told me later he remembered the warning and started crawling blindly til he found it at the edge of the bridge and slowly with his left hand he felt blindly and found the rut and started up the hill. We both knew the rut went all the way up. So… there we are with a beer and literally no sound. After about ½ an hour Cheech said "let's give him 20 more minutes and then we'll go get him". Maybe 10 minutes go by and we hear someone walking towards the Dome. In walks Billy, covered in mud and soaked to the skin. He calmly walks over to the fridge, pulls out a beer, sits down, looks up and says "How you boys doin?" One of the best laughs and my favorite story about my friend. There were many, many more but as I said at the top, some were bad, most were good, I picked this one because it was and still is one of my favorites. I loved him like a second brother and I always will.

# CHRISTIANSTED (PHASE 3) (BACK TO C'STED)

The next four or five years have sort of melted in my mind as we continued life on the island (and also back home) in mostly the same fashion. I have stories from this period but I can't actually put them in any chronological order so I will just write the highlights (and low) of this particular stretch of the journey.

One recollection (as I said these will probably not be in any datable order) was Danny's first trip. He had never really been away from New England, he was dating his future wife and he was not handling the island well. It got so bad I said ok, let's get someone to come down and take your place and that seemed to ease some of the pressure off his shoulders. I told him it would take a week or so, so he had to hang in there. The Grandstand Play was jammed every night and it was a gas. Around the third night and more than a few drinks, Danny seemed to be having a much better time. After every gig, which ended at 2 a.m. we would all go down to this little bar behind the club called the Hamilton Mews. Everyone still awake in town would always go there because everything else had closed down. Danny comes up and says "Hey, I don't think I want to go home". I was pretty sure that would be the way it would go so I actually hadn't even looked for anyone. We had been there 2 or 3 years before this and

I just thought he'd come around. Some time later that trip after a gig we were all heading down the Mews and Danny fell (it was one of those 5 minute torrential rains that came and went) and he probably broke his ankle, but we had no way to deal with it (Medical facilities were not really an option, especially at 3 in the morning. So we helped him back to the band house and the next morning it looked even worse. I said you're gonna have to play on a barstool. So, we started the night with Danny sitting, Once again, alcohol was involved... Sometime in the 2nd or 3rd set I looked over and Danny was standing up, playing while hopping on one foot. That was when I knew Danny was here to stay.

---

# IRISH JACK/ALPHONZO/ PHIL & THE STORM

This one, to be told correctly, spans a few years in the telling. It's truly a great story and I will be as concise as possible but due to the years and the characters involved it might take a little time. The first club we played in C'sted was called Pearl's and we went directly from the Strand across island to play there. They were actually as I said earlier in these stories building rooms above the club for the band and as I also said we called it the "Plywood Palace"... (Dianne loved it... not so much). Anyway, there was an old timer who cleaned up after the gig for drinks and whatever anyone who knew his plight could spare. His name was "Irish Jack", with a big hawk nose and a look that was, for lack of a better term, mischievous. He was one of many street people at the time but full of stories that I loved to listen to almost every night. He was on the island for a few seasons and suddenly on day he was gone. I asked around to all the locals but no one had any clue as to what happened. As often it does, the homeless can be lost down there without anyone noticing or paying any attention. So, fast forward a few years to Danny in the band and us moving up to the Grandstand. On any given night, there was no way of knowing what might happen... I mean anything was possible, Our next character in this tale is a fella named Alphonzo. He also was probably homeless, but he had a couple who owned a small bar in town called The Bilge, named Sarge and Candy. They seemed to keep an eye on him and help when it was needed. He was a round, big man, always smiling. I don't think I ever saw him mad, He had a red shirt with the word "Lithium" across the front. Swear to God, Sarge said it was to make sure he took the medicine, which is probably why he was always smilin'. He called Dianne "my little sweetie" and above it all he was a kind soul. The club that night was packed. You could barely move even on the dance floor. Dianne always had one of those Citronella candles on her piano (for the bugs, I think). Anyway the place was rockin and Alphonzo had a way of movin through the crowd, laughin and bumping into folks (mostly the girls) He's howling right in front of Dianne and suddenly he picks up the candle high above his head and pours the candle wax all over his face and mouth, howls again and shuffles back into the crowd. He had a big curly blond beard but the band watched in disbelief and tried to keep playing. So… As that was happening another well respected member of the Saint Croix community (I'm purposely leaving last names out here), Phil, the owner of the most popular beach on the West End already part of our F'staed time called Rainbow Beach, who we knew so well, having spent most of our first three months on the island out West and on his beach, was suddenly crawling along the floor towards the stage and specifically in Dianne's direction. She is unaware of him and he crawls up on the stage and starts biting her ankles!! In his defense it was nibbling more than actually biting. She screams, while everyone else was trying their level best not to bust out laughing. Crowd loved it, (perhaps this was not his first nibbling) and once Dianne realized it was Phil, I believe she either hit or kicked him, while he was laughing all the time. Just another night at the gig… So, the last set ends and Dianne, Danny and me find ourselves sitting on the steps below the club while torrential rain is rolling thru. These are the kinds of rains where your totally drenched two steps into it. Now to paint the picture correctly the walkways of Christiansted were built sometime in the 1700s. They are stone and brick and rounded at the top to make it similar to a series of archways. We are under the one closest to the ocean and the road home and we found ourselves sitting on the steps below the club while the rain is rolling thru. are under the one closest to the ocean and the road home. So, in the middle of this tropical downpour, we suddenly see Alphonzo come around the corner, smiling and humming a song to himself like it was a beautiful sunny day. He walks up to us and says "it's raining". One of us acknowledged he was right and he turns to leave back into the storm. He stops, turns and walks back to Dianne and says" Hey Sweetie, thanks for the candle wax" smiles that quirky, unique smile, and walks back into the rain leaving the three of us to ponder both his and our current situation... but the evening was not quite complete. I will take you back to the beginning of this particular story. I happened to look back up the walkway and in haze suddenly a lone figure steps out, big hawk nose. Danny didn't know him but Dianne and I did. I said "That's Jack!!" We got up and ran thru the walkways, getting drenched crossing each little break in the archways, and got up to him and said "Jack! You're back!" He looked at me, I think it took him a few seconds to remember me, but then he smiled and said "I'm looking for a red headed firebrand named McGillicuddy! I had no answer, being in a slight state of shock over the last few minutes of our lives. Then he says "if you see her tell Jack is back!". He turned and laughing, much the same as Alphonzo a few minutes earlier and walked out into the storm. We never saw him again... It was like a ghost had come and gone. Asked around for the next couple of days to the locals and no one but us had seen him,... then or since...

# FIGHTS IN THE BARS

No matter which bar we played in there were always fights. I won't go into detail on many, I'll just use this one (a particularly good one) as representative of the culture that the bar kids lived in. And by kids, I mean anyone from 15 to 50... So, on any given night the club was filled with about half locals and half tourists. I noticed this one couple who came in with what appeared to be a large Cruzan bodyguard. I had seen him on island before but never accompanying any one from stateside. The couple turned out to be this Texas oil guy (as I later found out) and the lady with him who was stunning. Blonde hair, blue eyes and as close to as pretty as any human can be ( at least in my opinion) . So they sit down at a table right next to the dance floor. I then see this local guy who I had seen often enough to know a litle bit about him. Big guy, 6'4" or so, and heard he used to play tight end for Penn State. I guess football or college didn't work out for him so again, as I have said before, here he was on St. Croix. It just so happened that week Dianne's sister Lisa and two of her friends had come down to visit and were sitting at a table up front next to us. Penn State is at the bar pretty well on his alcohol way and he sees our beautiful blonde. At this point I need to tell a side story which will come into play. We had just gotten a top of the line piano for Dianne called a CP-70. It was used by every major player at the time and we really couldn't afford it, but we bought it anyway. Now, I see Penn State heading towards Texas, his lady and our Cruzan friend. I've been here awhile and this had real trouble written all over it. So he walks over and appears to ask her to dance to which she politely declines. He goes back to the bar where his friends are havin some real fun at his expense. Bright bunch of guys. So… Penn State walks back to the table, as I say on mic to Lisa and her friends to "get on the stage now!' They pick up their drinks and move from the table just as the Cruzan bodyguard sends our local football hero right through Lisa's table. Now as a rule, bar fights are fast and over quickly but the local friends with him get into it and now we've got a Texas/Cruzan vs. Local drunks melee rollin around on the floor, At the time my Mic stand had what was called an Atlas base made of solid iron. The band had stopped playing and as calmly as I could over the sound system I said to stay away from the stage but mostly I meant the piano. We still owed like $5,000 on it. So I stood with the mic stand base in front and gently (well, not so sort of gently) hit anybody within two feet of me, and I could tell from my first intruder this thing hurt like hell. I must have tapped (well, sort of tapped) seven or eight guys before they got the idea and by then bartenders, and the bouncer had pulled them apart and threw everybody out of the bar. We took a break while the Grandstand folks tried to put the bar back in order and I'm standing outside the club and I see them let Texas and his group back in the bar… then I see them let the Penn State team back in. So… I go running back to the piano just in time to see them go at it again, and man my mic-stand post while we relived the standard dumb STX episode of 10 minutes earlier one more time… Yep, that's my island.

••◄━━━━●━━━━►••

# THE DAY I QUIT DRINKING SCOTCH

Ok, this will take a little revisit involving an earlier time line already touched on in my story. When I was in Up With People I never drank. I got kicked out at 19-20 years old for reasons I have again already written about earlier, and as it happened the effect was devastating and I spiraled down. I did (again as I have said before, pulled out of it), but you never really just "pull out of it". So, we need to go back to where my family came from. We were Irish Catholic, and so was everyone else in our entire neighborhood. My Mom carried very little weight and my Dad was the one who we'd follow. Everybody drank in the family, at parties, or ballgames or holidays, or weekends, or whenever... so we in the younger generation, all growing up together did not see it as any sort of an issue. As I have said before, I had a few beers in high school after Stamford High won a ballgame, even a few times after we lost. Didn't matter the sport, Port Chester was 10 miles away. Drinking age was 21 in Connecticut it was18 in NY, so it was never really a big deal. Fast forward to post UWP and my personal loss of purpose and direction. I have talked about this earlier but not in relation to alcohol. It happens slowly and, at least for me, it was not an aware realization that I was getting deeper into drinking, and at the time felt no danger or fear of it. As I proceeded playing music, first as a soloist and later in our various bands, I think I just followed along without any awareness of trouble. As I moved into better players and eventually to Dianne and Danny and we were experiencing success and growing in confidence so it became part of the process. Now, back to my issues with performing and alcohol. I started out in the gigs with beer but over the next few years I moved on to scotch. At first, it had no major effect on me or my relationship with my future wife, my brother or anyone else playing with us. However, once we started playing on St. Croix regularly and really were becoming the main event on island every night, houses of stateside tourists and locals who were always amazing, interesting and well, there, night after night, good or bad, we became the place to be. So I think what happened to me was I became immune to anything that interfered with the status of every wonderful night after night. In retrospect I'm sure this cost me dearly, and also our climb up of what have been the mountain... Make no mistake, it was my fault, not Dianne's or Danny's... it was mine. When you're so full of yourself it's easy to be self-absorbed and stupid. Eventually we reached a point where I was... for lack of any defense... out of control. I remember it was a night, much like all the others, but there had been a murder in town, I'll say that again.. a murder in town which of course rarely happened, and everyone local was on edge... I was particularly off depending on any perspective that others might find reasonable and I remember pissing Dianne of , so bad that as we finished the gig, it's 2:30 in the morning, and me, Dianne and Danny were out in the parking lot by the pier, and Dianne was real busy telling me what a true jerk I was, she also had Danny on her side, swinging her purse at me and screaming, and yes ..screaming at me... now let's go back to the fact that in town was the "murderer", a local Puerto Rican man, well known to police and locals, alike, who was being sought by the government authorities. At that moment he came out of the shadows and said, and I quote, "Hey man, you got to calm down, you're gonna bring the cops down here!! And Dianne looks at me and said one of the most memorable statements in all of our lives..,

she said, "Great!!, The Murderer!!!, is telling you to calm down!!!"
I still, remembering how I would not back down. Total fool... so,
thru the blur of it all, we went back to the band house just like
every other night and went to bed. I woke up sometime around
noon, with the whole band sitting at the edge of my bed... this
did not look good. Add that to the fact that I went to bed pretty
well done and it took a moment to focus on what appeared to be a
possible problem. It wasn't just Dianne or Danny, it was the whole
band and Perry Cavari, our drummer said, "Dave, I love playing
with you, but if you don't stop drinking Scotch, I'm done... and
so is everyone else." I was in no position to even try and mount
a credible defense, plus the fact that I knew they were right. So
I said" Okay, I'll try" and Danny or Dianne, (I can't remember
which, said) "No, if you don't stop we're all done". So, this was a
very bad day for Dave, or maybe the first step (baby step) back for
me. That night I started drinking beer on ice and though it truly
wasn't easy, it also was not that bad. There were moments when I
said to myself, I can't hold the crowd, the excitement level... MY
excitement level. And this, in the way I saw myself and the room
as possibly altering either who I was, or at least how I saw myself,
in relationship to the music and the nightly performance of that
music. But I stayed that course and the crowd, didn't change and it
was my true first step back to why I am still here and lucky enough
to be writing this for my grandchildren. There are other Demons
of mine up the road but I will leave that for another story, but is
an essential part of this particular period of our time on STX, and
in retrospect it leveled my ship. And the band didn't leave, thank
you guys, but mostly thank you Dianne and Danny.

⊷⬦⊶⬦⊷

# CONNECTICUT, NEW YORK CITY AND MARRIAGE

All during our time down south we continued to pursue a national career and being so close to the City we began playing many of the popular venues in New York. This involved playing gigs at all hours of the night, because New York is truly the City that never sleeps. This didn't really fit with Dianne's lifestyle but she did it heroically for a number of years. But we were older now and in the life span of a pop/rock band we were getting to the end of that period quickly. Dianne and I had been the closest of friends and it slowly became clear to me that she was the best person I had ever known, but I was not ready for any commitment, so a few rather strange years went by where we were together and then apart and than again together over and over. Finally, Dianne said she had an offer to move to California to work for her uncle who at that time was the CEO of SONY. I could not see my life without her. So in a restaurant called Le Chateau, our favorite restaurant, I asked her to marry me. It was and still is the best thing that's ever happened to me. Now Dianne's parents had eloped because she was Jewish and Tony, Italian and in Brooklyn back then was unacceptable to Dixie's family, so they never had a real wedding. Well, ours quickly became hers. They planned for only the best, from a Bentley bringing her to the church to 300 plus guests of which I knew about 50. It was a such a great event. All who had been there would agree. Our honeymoon started in Rome and ended a month later in Paris. We spent the second half with our friends Albert and Sarah Bouchard meeting us in Saint Tropez and Albert, being the head chef at Le Chateau, took us thru the Alps from one amazing restaurant to another all the way to Paris. Life returned pretty much back to normal. Of course Jenna and 8 years later Kate would have a lot to say as to how our lives would change. We continued to go to the island year after year as a duo and I really had no idea how or what our next chapter would be.

⋅⋅◀▬▬▬▬▬●▬▬▬▬▬▶⋅⋅

# HUGO

The island went along at pretty much the same place as when we first arrived some 10 years earlier, with amazing crowds night after night, and lazy days on the beaches every day. St. Croix was something to see back then… streets filled with people, at least 10 music venues from folk to reggae, jazz and the three main clubs, Truly a tourist driven island. When we left in the summer of 1988 I had no idea what was going to happen. Dianne was pregnant with Jenna and I was unsure how it would affect our lives. She was born in late December of 88, so for the first year since she arrived and we didn't go. Being a father wasn't really registering with me. I just assumed she was coming along for the ride, (which in the end is exactly what happened) but there came a life altering natural event in September of 1989 that would not only change our lives but the lives of every single person living on St. Croix. A storm was forming in the Atlantic and moving toward the islands. It grew into one of the most massive hurricanes ever recorded. Hugo. The initial path looked like it would pass us to the south. But, as it moved through the islands farther down the chain and into the warm waters of the Caribbean Sea, it began to swing more northerly. Most people probably don't know but the deadliest part of these storms are not very big. A miss of 40 miles from the center can hurt you for sure, but not crush you. The closer it got the Virgin Islands the more it looked increasingly bad. As we watched from Connecticut, with so many friends on island it became apparent we were about to see something horrific. Hugo made a direct landfall around sunset with sustained winds of 185 mph and gusts of up to 250 mph. No hurricane before or since had the force of this storm. The eye came directly over the island in the middle of the night and as it went over and maybe an hour later the winds returned from the opposite direction. In the morning as it was finally passing there was not a power pole left standing, not a house undamaged and it looked like a nuclear bomb had hit it. There was no power anywhere on the island for 6-9 months, and it would take years to rebuild. The St. Croix we left was no longer there and has never been the same since. Yes, after 4 or five years houses were rebuilt and life went on, but never again did it return to the place that it had been. It is now a truly beautiful island again, but the tourist industry never recovered. I returned the following year after the storm without Dianne or Jenna, It was still just destroyed and dangerous. It had been 16 months since the storm and much of the island was still without power. I played in a little club called Hondo's Backyard, almost entirely to FEMA, electricians, plumbers, roofers and the National Guard. Coolers filled with beer was the only drink available. There was an 8 o'clock mandatory curfew and everyone needed to be off the streets by then. So at 7:30 I would close down, turn off the generator and start again at 4:30 the next day. Going around the island was one of the worst experiences of my life. It had been well over a year and it still looked like a war zone. Houses crushed, power lines still down, and everything I had known was gone. I could go on about it, but I'm fairly sure this was the actual state for some time and which very, very slowly came back. As I said we came back every year but played to a much smaller crowd in much smaller rooms. The three main clubs never opened again as there was no one really to support those size of venues. I'll leave the Hugo story now and move past it to the new reality of St. Croix.

# POST HUGO

We found a new home to play the following year. It was located in the Caravelle Hotel on the water in C'sted. It went thru many names over the first number of years but eventually a family, the McCulloughs (three brothers, and two wives) brought the know how to make it work and it became Rumrunners. Our deal with the owner of the hotel was a room and one meal, five nights a week playing and we luckily became again the main attraction in town. As it had changed hands so many times, when we got on island I got us situated in Room 208, which become our home for many years. The hotel was run by Elsie Galaway (manager), Joyce, Louis and Christina all local Cruzan folks, "bon(born) and raised" who each carried on their duties that made the engine run. I brought the sound system down to set up. As I was doing so a young man came up to me and asked if he could help me. I said that was very kind but I was fine. He then asked "Who are you?". I told him and I said, "Who are you?", to which he replied "My name is Chris McCullough and I own this restaurant". So, obviously a fork in the road was about to be crossed. I gave him our history in the room and asked if we could play one night. If he liked it, we'd stay, if not, we'd go. He said okay and thanks to God the place was packed with locals and tourists and their response (it being our first night back on island) was very positive. That was 21 years ago, and we have there ever since. Jenna was probably three or four, and while we played Louis and Christina would take her with them, in the office (Christina) or around the grounds (Louis). They would become both Jenna and later Kate's Godparents while we were there. A deep love still beats in all their hearts to this day.

---

# LIFE IN CHRISTIANSTED WITH THE KIDS:

With no daily vehicle our lives revolved around the beach in the day and the gigs at night. As I have said earlier there is a small island just off shore of town with a time share residents, a restaurant/bar and a beautiful beach called Hotel on the Cay. You took a small ferry over and back and we spent most of our days there as we had as a much younger group of musicians. Jenna was still a baby and we had portable crib which the bartender Errol was kind to us and kept it behind the bar. To understand the dynamic of this small community on this little island just offshore you have to understand that same people came down to their timeshare every year so everyone knew everyone else. Every few weeks another group of friends would come so Jenna being the only child, these folks knew her and she grew up with a bunch of quasi aunts and uncles who truly loved her and watching her grow up. The same thing happened with Kate eight years later which made their lives filled with folks who treated them as their own. Again as I said, the Cay was inside the reef so to water was more like a calm lake as opposed to the open ocean with waves and currents. For the girls this made it an ideal and safe environment which was great for all of us. We had convinced the Stamford school system to allow us to home school them and that went well for many years and I believe it gave them a unique way to grow up and see many people from many countries and all over the USA. This long stretch of time has very few stories which in itself can be a good thing. As Jenna got older (4 or 5) she began to sing with us (which of course was the highlight of any evening to both locals and tourists) and as Kate came along she did the same. I do have a few memories of interest that are worth sharing.

This first one shows the level of the Cruzan culture and the American presence on the island. Inside the town there was never a feeling of danger. Now, as with any place, if you went out of a certain part of town you could find yourself in some bad situations. But not in town and especially in the Caravelle. We had some friends from the states on island and we were sitting up on a terrace when three young Cruzan boys came up. This rang all sorts of bells and I said to everyone it was time to go. It was a tense moment but they let them go probably because Jenna and our friends daughter Julia were there. I told them I was staying there and lets just let everyone go first. I had no intention of fighting three 18 year olds, so as soon as everyone was gone I followed as fast as I could, ran into the restaurant and told them to watch out cause they were inside the courtyard of the Caravelle. Our friends and Dianne and Jenna went back to their rooms and as I came out the into the courtyard as the Cruzan kids were also coming into the same space. Our rooms were up the stairs on the second floor I wouldn't go to the room but the stairs had side rails so it gave me an advantage cause there was only one way up. I then saw one of them had a knife and said to them "you can't do this! There's no way out!". I was getting prepared from being above them to use my legs to defend my position, as that was the best I could think of. At that exact moment Elsie barreled into the boys saying "What you doin in my hotel?" I said "Elsie he has a knife!!" she continued walking them backwards and I watched as three dangerous young men turn into boys being scolded by their Grandmother. It was astounding. She bullied them right out of the hotel and back into the street. I said "How'd you do that?", She replied that if they hurt me in town they would not live out the night. She said "I know these boys and they know me". I thanked her and felt a little like she was a grandmother to me too. This was a very rare incident so my goal is to learn or teach the amount of respect I have for this Cruzan culture.

Another defining moment and very different one between Cruzan and American culture came one morning at The Caravelle. Staying there for months at a time we became very close to all who worked there. One of the ladies who cleaned the rooms name was Ms. Eileen... You can imagine 4 people in a single room for months at a time, there can be some bickering, arguing and general family stuff. Dianne left for coffee in the restaurant (probably just to get away for a moment to herself). And it should noted that all of these wonderful ladies were always so kind and gracious to us. As Dianne greeted Ms. Eileen she asked how she was and Ms Eileen replied "I am blessed, and you?". Dianne said "I'm just going to get some coffee cause they're all in there arguing". To which Ms. Eileen replied "It is good to have someone to argue with". Well, I'm not sure how Dianne reacted but when she told me what happened we both agreed this was a gift of wisdom and grace and learning a valuable life lesson can be found simply in any moment. I have never forgotten this beautiful story. Or Ms. Eileen...

# HURRICANE MARIA, NOT HUGO BUT... AND THE GOODNESS FOUND INSIDE A SOUL

As years passed in our lives and on the island, needless to say we had learned much especially how fragile life and nature could be. Hugo was in '89 and we had brushes with other hurricanes but to truly understand these storms the devastation really only reaches out 20-25 miles from the eye and after that it just becomes a wicked storm. So, almost 20 years later after Hugo, we had bought our condo overlooking the St. Croix harbor making the island officially our second home and if you are lucky enough to own property there you watch the weather closely. So in mid September, 2017 two storms formed in the Atlantic moving towards the islands. Hurricanes Irma and Maria. Rarely do you see two storms moving simultaneously towards us. As they got closer they both were not changing paths. Irma hit St. Thomas, St. John and the British Virgin Islands passing us to the north. However, Maria was moving south towards St. Croix. It passed seven miles south but well within the range to do serious destruction, which it did. We watched helplessly as the storm tore through the island. It surely wasn't at the level of Hugo, but it was still a terribly ruthless storm. Power again was out for, no one could say how long, but it was going to be long. Our home was shielded by a mountain dividing the Schooner Bay complex. On the east side the homes unprotected from the mountain were basically destroyed. On our side, under the cover of this large piece of land we were basically unscathed. I spoke to our Condo manager Jonathan and he said he went in and we were alright but he also said how bad the damage was on the exposed side. So flights were down for some time. I flew down about a month after the storm and my dear friend Louis who keeps my car while I am off island met me the airport and immediately the situation was obvious. No baggage claim, no power anywhere, no traffic lights and on and on. I got to the condo as the sun was setting and I realized I was soon to be in the dark. My neighbor Beth Swazey brought me flashlights and an amazing amount of toys to make it possible to see without power. The next day was a bad, bad day. The condo was as Jonathan said was basically fine except for six inches of mud and debris on the patio. I was thankful for that good fortune but also aware how much of the island and it's people had lost. I had my car so I could drive around to see how it really was and it was terrible. All power lines down, small houses destroyed and just destruction after destruction. There was one grocery store open on a generator and again my gratitude to Jonathan to tell me cash was the only currency. No power. I brought down a large amount of cash and had maybe $700 in my wallet. Luckily our original home at the Caravelle Hotel was also on a generator so I could charge my phone and stay within communication on the island. The cell towers had been damaged so there was no way to reach the mainland or anyplace else for that matter but somehow communicating on the island was still possible. I couldn't call Connecticut so I was more on my own than I realized. I think it was the third day when I went to the grocery store (Beth had left me some basics) and a lot of the locals had trucks that made local food to eat. So the Grocery was called Pueblo and I got things that did not need refrigeration, paid in cash and went on my way. My next stop was the Library which was open but basically just letting people take books on the honor system. I instinctively reached for my wallet for my library card and realized it was gone. Panic... ran out to the car, nothing. Got in the car and tore back to the Pueblo parking lot, than into the store. Again nothing. I came to to the fact that it was gone, and gone for good. The money was one thing but everything in the wallet was much more important, especially my license which was my only means of identification. I went back to the condo and eventually rationalized the situation. Whoever found it needed the money more than I did and I would just have to make my way forward. By the time I went to bed, I think I was actually okay with what had happened. So, at some moment I hear my phone doing what phones do. I reach over to a messenger message saying "are you David Gunnip?". I obviously say "Yes" and then it replies " I am Sargent Ford from the Frederiksted Police Department and I have your wallet". Well now I'm wide awake and say "My wallet?" (I know, sharp as a tack right?, but let's remember I'm totally disoriented and was asleep) he asks me my birthday I answer and I ask" is anything in it?" he laughs and says "hell yes, a bunch of money, credit cards and your license". I asked if I could come now and get it and he says "sure" and tells me where the police station is. Having basically grown up in F'sted I knew so I said "Thank You, I'm on my way!" He laughed again and said "Don't rush, I'm here all night!". I get in the car and it's a drive all the way across the island from East to West so 25 minutes later I at the F'sted police station. I walk in to see Sargent Ford at his desk. He looks at me and says "yes, that's you" with my license in his hand. He hands me my wallet and there is nothing, and I mean nothing missing. I was past stunned I said "who did this?" he smiled and said her name is Anna Simone, she lives on Mahogany Road in" and I stopped him and said "in the rain forest". He said "yes, how did you know?" I told him I lived above the wood shop" and he then stopped me and said "Leap?, I then smiled and said ,"Cheech?" and his smile was wider than mine and he said, "it is such a small world". I thought I knew where she lived and I was right . There was a small community just past Leap and he comfirmed it. He then said" you can't go there because most of the homes are gone". I said I'll go tomorrow and he asked if I had a four wheel vehicle which I did and he said "tell Anna Terrence says hello". So, you can't do the rain forest at night, especially after a hurricane, so I go home. In the morning I head back out West pull onto Mahagony Road past Leap and find the road (if you can call it that) and head up to where I find a group of Cruzan people basically living outside on cots on land. I'm again stunned. I park and ask "does anyone know Anna Simone" and this beautiful older Cruzan women says "I'm Anna". I'm usually pretty good with words but I swear I was speechless. I said "you found my wallet?". She beamed and said "Yes, I'm so happy they found you!!". Again, nothing... I then said, "I don't know how to thank you, please take the money because you saved me from so much!". She looked at me quizzically and said "No, that is your money" I tried to explain what she had done for me but she was adamant. "God would never allow me that" . I tried to process but I had learned a lot about the Cruzan culture so I then asked "Can I give you a reward for helping me?" She beamed again and said "the reward is returning your property to you". So now I'm in the presence of a much older soul than me and I'm thinking... " I say "would God let you accept a gift?". She stared at me for a long time and then quietly replied "Yes". Took out all the money and she put up her hand in a stop motion. I took half the money and said "half for me and half for you as a gift to you and all these people". She looked hard at me and just said thank you. I left feeling I had been in the presence of someone on a much, much deeper level of knowledge than I might ever know. I still feel that today as I am writing down this story down.

# MY DAD AND JENNA

When Jenna was born, we had a crowd in the waiting room, and I mean a crowd, probably 25 people. Now a short point before the story. All my life I had heard my parents refer to themselves as "Mom" and "Dad". My mother had gone to the cafeteria with Dianne's sister Susan, and they were gone when they brought Jenna out. My Dad said "oh no, she's gonna miss it!" At that moment my mother and Susan came around the corner and he said "C'mere Gram, she's here!!" from that instant on they called each other "Gram" and "Gramp". It was a seamless transition that to this day I don't think they even realized it, but it was not lost on me and it's one of my most precious memories of my parents. My father invented ways to be at our house every day just to see Jenna. Didn't matter what it was, he would make up things to do. Don't misunderstand me my Mom loved her too, but I had never witnessed that depth of love that my Dad had for Jenna. She grew up surrounded by family and was raised by a village. As we at that time were still full time musicians she would stay with my parents, Dianne's parents or her sister Lisa. She was a beautiful soft soul from the day she was born. As with most tales when nothing bad or strange happens there isn't much to say and that was the case with Jenna. She, to this day is the same caring person she was as a child. We continued on in this unique lifestyle of winters in the

Caribbean and the rest of our time in Connecticut and still be able to continue to play music as a lifelong blessing and passion.

## STORY #50

•••◆•◆━━━━━━◆━━━━━━◆•◆•••

# DAD

U p to this point in the story I have talked about my Dad in great lengths as he related to me, and my family. I never really talked about just him… I wasn't there but I've been told and know in my heart that he did it all. He grew up in a house with 17 kids. His Mom died when he was three and his Aunt Nell and Pop took them in. Three weeks later Nell's other sister died (both I believe, deep flu or pneumonia) and with her 12 kids, and my grandfather's three and his aunt's two left Nell to deal with 17 children ever day. At seventeen he lied about his age and went to war with every other man or boy and never spoke about it til the real very end of his life. He had a chance to try out for the Detroit Lions as a pitcher,… He was that good. He lived thru numerous landings in North Africa, piloting the amphibious boats that brought the soldiers to shore. For many miles each time, he and his fellow drivers of these crafts were the only targets the Germans had to shoot at. After four years, like so many of the lucky ones he came home. His returning dream was to contact the Detroit Tigers scout only to be told at 21 he was too old… that should have broken many boys/men dream. I wasn't there and I didn't know about this until he saw my love of sports and told me this story and it gave me the belief that I could reach that level mostly in baseball but actually all sports now as I look back. He remains to this day my hero…

# KATE

Now the tale grows interesting again… It was seven years after Jenna was born, the three of us living in the same room at the Caravelle and Dianne walks into the room and says "I just heard a song called "The Only Child". As with most great country songs it will find its particular way to pull your heartstrings. She then said "Jenna shouldn't be an only child" I mentioned we were now in our early 40s and that might be worth thinking about. Well, we did but Dianne in the end was bent on this so… sure enough within a short time she announced to the family that another child was joining the team. Now, even before Kate was born she was making her presence felt. She arrived more than two months early and weighed less than two pounds. You could literally hold her in your hand. She started her adventures in the children's ICU. My concerns were many and mostly dark. Would she be blind, deaf or suffer brain damage were right at the top of a long list. The unit was open to parents 24/7 so while Dianne was recuperating I was out playing in the clubs, mostly solo. Every night after the gigs I would go to the hospital and sit there from 1-3. I finally got the courage up to ask one of the nurses what her chances were. She smiled at me and said "this child is going to be fine, but what a temper she has!". I didn't understand so she told me they put a tube up her nose for oxygen and every time they did and came back around to check she had pulled it out. She said, and I'll never forget it "you better be ready cause she's gonna give you a run for your money". Little did I know how spot on she was. We brought here home about a month later after she got up to 4 pounds. And just as with Jenna, she had round the clock care from the same village that raised Jenna. To this very day I will never understand how two sisters both raised the same way could go in completely different directions... I love them both the same and always will, but boy was her nurse right. She was stubborn, willful and angry if things didn't go her way. "It's a phase" Dianne's mother would say... Well so far, it's a 26 year phase with little possibility of it changing any time soon that I have seen. So let's visit a few early Kate stories... every year among our regular gigs we would do many concerts either by ourselves or opening for various national recording acts. On this particular date we were opening for the band "America", a very well known group at the time at an event known as "The Oyster Festival". We had been playing this event for many years. Jenna who was now 12 would join us in these types of venues and any crowd loves to hear a child sing, and Jenna could really sing. There were probably 10,000 or more there that night but it was only Kate's first time backstage. Let's remember she is 4. We finish a song and Kate walks right on stage. I said,"Hi Kate, what's up" to which she replies, "I want to sing a song" To backtrack just a bit, there was always music in our house so Kate was just used to it and to us singing together. But also let's remember, a huge crowd, a big stage... I said" What would you like to sing?", I think my Dad taught it to her and she said, "Take me out to the ballgame" I put her on my lap and away she went! Dianne, who has perfect pitch immediately began to play behind her. Kate was spot on and received a standing ovation, jumped off my lap, smiled and walked off stage. I don't remember what we played following her performance, but we had been upstaged and I still to this day couldn't be prouder of her. They both continue to sing and when they sing with us nothing makes me happier.

Another Kate created story is an amazing look back for me. Out East on the island on top of one of one of the mountains was a place known only as "The Castle". No one we knew had ever been there. It was owned by a mysterious women known only as "The Contessa". You can see the castle from the road and it looked every bit like a one. A huge marble structure that as I have later learned she had it built specifically from a European property that she once saw and loved. Now once in a great while we would splurge and go to a restaurant called The Terrace located at the Buccaneer Resort. The girls were all dressed up and this was our big night out. Jenna was twelve and Kate was four. From our table we watched as an entourage led by this elegant woman swept into the room. Our waitress, Ruby, whispered "that's the Contessa!". She was followed by at least 4 men all of them dressed in black including the Contessa… Kate, who as always been very vocal and willing to, without intimidation or fear, speak her mind. She said "I'd like to meet her" I said "Kate?"… And then I thought, why not? I asked Jenna if she would walk Kate over to their table, and she said "Sure". My two girls walked to their table and Dianne and I watched for the next five minutes as they talk directly to the Contessa. They eventually returned and came back to the table. I said "How was it?" and Jenna said "Great, she's really nice!". A moment later one of the gentleman from her table and I can't explain but I knew immediately this was her main consort said "I am Yuri… and the Contessa would like to invite you to lunch tomorrow". Well, that was something… and Kate was smiling the whole time, and so was Jenna. We gladly accepted and actually went over to thank her personally and she was charming and gracious and said she looked forward to our time tomorrow. So we were given directions to the road which led up to the castle, rented a Jeep and found ourselves on the way to the Castle. At the top of the hill waiting behind a wrought iron gate was Yuri with two big Dobermans and he was made it clear that they were well behaved so we followed him up.. And it was just that… a castle. All in marble and immaculately decorated, with a beautiful white grand piano and a dome in the main room that rose maybe 60 feet up. She explained there were only four rooms in this immense structure The Living room, her bedroom, an amazing dining room and guest room. Yuri explained that there were many servants quarters below and took us on a tour of the grounds and they were spectacular. From the top of the mountain, you had both views, east and west of the island unlike any I had ever seen. We then returned to the Countess and she said "Yuri, we would love lunch please" He answered "Yes Countess" (a phrase we heard at least 25 times during the afternoon). Needless to say the meal was wonderful, but for the life of me I couldn't tell you what it was. She appeared to have some slight memory lapses, as she asked Yuri a number of requests which she had already asked. Yuri's voice never changed, he never corrected her and showed total patience and respect. She told us of her life, 5 husbands, one a Count (hence the Countess), while she was having a joyous moment with Dianne and the girls, I quietly asked Yuri if this was her main home. He smiled and said" Oh no, this is her winter residence. She has four other homes, but the main house is in South Hampton in Long Island". She was quiet candid in describing her various husbands implying one was more wealthy than next and on and on. There was a portrait of her in her youth and she was really quite beautiful. She still was and she was well into her seventies. We told her our story of our time on the island and she was so interested in listening I just found her one of the most unique person I've ever spent time with. As with many of our family rollercoaster rides, it all started with Kate!

———•———

# APPLE VALLEY: PRIDE AND MISSING THE POINT

All our lives we had been blessed making money in so many various ways from commercials to studio work with many very talented and amazing national musicians as well as being on many concert stages. Our first house was great and have nothing but wonderful memories from there. Still, I wanted to move to a home that I thought would be one that I and particularly my parents would be proud of. My folks had come from very, very poor and I wanted them to see what we had accomplished. I found an absolutely beautiful home on three acres of land and overlooking an amazing lake in the woods at the very top of our town near the New York State line. We had families of deer, foxes and various wildlife in our back yard every day. It really was my dream house. However, I never thought that the kids, especially Kate, might respond differently. She had lived her whole life in a wonderful neighborhood just doors down from Dianne's parents and minutes from ours. This new house was much farther from everyone and what I thought had beauty and seclusion became more of a prison for Kate. To her, I began to realize, the change had taken much in her life away. No matter how we tried it became more and more clear that she was unhappy and became what eventually was one of my worst decisions. Dianne's sister Lisa and her partner Erin still lived in our old neighborhood and they had two dogs that Kate adored and she began to stay over their house on various days and it was obvious that she was much happier with the dogs and the neighborhood. Also getting to school which was a one minute ride from her aunts, which had turned from an hour plus ride because we had moved far from the school. Jenna was not unhappy with the house, but she could drive and had a much easier time dealing with the move. But Kate was not happy. Not knowing what to do, we began to let her stay with her aunts more and more, especially on school days. Without realizing it we were slowly losing Kate and it still is one of most regrettable choices I have ever made. I put what I wanted ahead of what my family needed. My only defense is that it never occurred to me that they would have a different perspective of it. As time moved on she began to have two homes. We would still, the four of us go to St. Croix every winter, continue playing music as a family and basically shared Kate with her aunts when we were home. Please understand they did and still do love her unconditionally, but I believe at this moment we all four of us lost hold of Kate and her stubborn and willful side began to emerge. This is not necessarily a bad thing because it's a part of her that I still love and admire, but she really had no one leading her train. Her schoolwork became erratic her behavior took on a more troubling direction. Things just seem to slide away from us. Tension between Dianne's sister and me became an issue, as we began to disagree on what was best for Kate and that, sadly remains to this day. Getting her through high school was done with mirrors and whistles, but she made it. So at this point in these tales, Kate is out of high school, and I will add has grown dramatically on her own into a beautiful young slightly crazy lady and Jenna is graduated from college with a Masters degree, married, with two beautiful children, Johnny and Rosie who I love more than words can ever express… so…

---

# THEIR STORIES: JENNA, KATE, JOHNNY AND ROSIE

As I'm editing this for it's final draft I had originally written five or six stories about them and each of their lives, when I suddenly realized that those are not my stories… they're their stories and hopefully someday will be told by them. They're really not mine to tell. As I read them, and make know mistake I believe they are good stories, and if you've come this far, it's clearly apparent that I am a story teller. But again, they are not my stories. I will however leave you with two last tales both happening to me in this past year, one in Connecticut and one on Saint Croix that hopefully will tie my time today and all these many stories into the context of a life. I hope you will find them both worthwhile…

━━━●━━━━●━━━━●━━━

# 2023: CONNECTICUT

So Dianne and I have been going to an Italian restaurant called Pellicci's for literally ever. Originally the whole neighborhood was a poor area of town and I spent a lot of time there as a boy. The road goes right by a large area of land run by the Woman's Club of Stamford which has three or four basketball hoops (half court) and below down a hill was a baseball field named after a famous local coach and umpire who worked with the kids in Stamford his whole life. It's called Mickey Lione Field. I truly can't tell you how many games I played there growing up. Today the field (though the infield is still there) is used mostly for soccer with literally hundreds of people playing on various parts of the space. On this day I was alone heading for the restaurant. I had plenty of time to kill and for some reason I pulled into the parking lot to watch the guys play B'ball. I was without a doubt the only old guy there. There were four courts, two with some kids just running around and shooting, the third court had older kids playing a decent game. But on the fourth court were all guys who could really play. Three on three, fast, tall and so worth watching. One point guard looked a step quicker than the rest and I found myself studying him and his moves. To remind you, I played in high school, used mostly in defense cause I was small for basketball (6 feet) but I was fast and could stay with the opposing teams point guard and used mostly in close games. A young man next to me said "you play?",

I smiled and said "I used to", he then said "any good?" with a grin. I replied "I was never a good shooter but I would have loved to have guarded him". He gave me this funny look and looked down at my flip flops.. He said "What size shoe?". Wasn't quite sure where he was headed and then he said "I'm am eleven". I said "Me too" Then he really smiled and yells out towards the court "Hey Reggie!!! This guy thinks he can guard you!!!", as he's taking his shoes off! Reggie smiles and says "yea sure". I'm staring at, whose name I later learned was Jerome, and must've looked stunned cause he said "It's cool , what's the worst that could happen?" I said " I could get killed!". But by now we had a bunch of kids looking to join in on the fun. I was stuck. Just like in our day it was shirts and skins and I thank God my team were the shirts, seriously. I put on Jerome's sneakers(barefoot) and walked out towards Reggie and said to him "I got a bad back and got maybe 5 or 10 minutes tops". He had one of the widest best smiles I've ever seen and said" that's ok, it wont take that long". So… Reggie ball out, me trying to guard him. He fakes left, I totally buy it and blows back past me to my right and scores without me even touching him, so, so much for my ego. Our ball, I'm at point. Now as I said I'm not a shooter but I know ball, and I can play. Reggie's closing in on me and my guy to the right fakes toward the basket and I look like I'm passing that way. Reggie leans planning to steal. My other teammate fakes out right and then back left and his guy goes with him as mine cuts towards the basket. Reggie's just a bit out of position. I bounce pass and catch him in full stride going by his man. Straight up dunk. (I did say these guys were big, right?). Reggie looks at me again with that same smile and says "Ok… Ok". But by now my backs already telling me time was quickly growing short. So Reggie has the ball and I looked right at him and I said "Not this time,.. not this time". Now I knew, and I can't explain why, he could have done the same exact drive on me and score with very little trouble with really nothing I could do. But the look in his eyes, and please understand, it was not a mean or angry look at all. But the challenge I saw said he just didn't want to beat me... He wanted to "beat me"... his ball, his court, and ninety nine times out of a hundred he would have. But I sensed a change coming. He started exactly like he did the first time, left than cut right I went left with him but didn't go back right. He cut back to the left to go around me the opposite way towards the basket but anyone who knows the game well knows he'd have to put the ball in his left hand to take it and make that pivot, and for that split second the ball is exposed. He crossed hands to his left and I reached out and tipped it and he lost control and the ball bounced back to one of my guys who stepped behind the arc and buried a three! He looked at me, I really can't find the words to describe the look... but it was genuine. We fist pumped and I said "I'm done, my back is killin me!", and then that smile again. He said "ain't no thing sir, but you still got it". Probably one of the best compliments I've ever received in my life. I looked back at him as I limped towards to Jerome and my flip flops and Reggie just pointed his finger at me and we both smiled. I thanked Jerome for the sneakers and he quietly said, "Man, you picked his pocket!!" also a great compliment. I drove to the restaurant, sat at the bar, and felt better than I have in such a very, very long time.... Great, great moment... 2023

# 2023: SAINT CROIX

So, a final short story. Here on the island we drive on the left. I'm driving our old Jeep Cherokee we have here back from setting up at Castaways. As I'm pulling up towards the red light. Let me just say often folks visiting from the states make the same mistake being unfamiliar to the opposite side of the road. a shiny new Jeep on the left of the intersection turns directly hard right heading directly at me... horn, horn, brakes... and inches. A local old Cruzan man siting on the curb waves toward the driver in his bright tropical shirt and smiling he says "Hey mon you're not from around here". He then turns to me and again smiling and waving... and we both just laughed. So I guess I get to play music once more, at least tonight... Cruzan culture and humor, it still cracks me up and boy I always feel lucky to be a part of it most of my life...

# TODAY

At this moment, I just turned 70, Dianne 68, My girls are in their 20's and 30's. Johnny is 7 and Rosie, 3. It goes without saying they are the light of Dianne's and my life and hopefully will be for a very long time. But one never knows what's up ahead and I pray that I will get to write a sequel with many more tales but at this time it appears I have come to the close of my stories. Thanks to anyone who stuck with me through this very long and varied set of tales. I am a lucky and grateful man. I have been blessed more the I ever deserved... I hope to see you all ten or fifteen years from now with more stories about Jenna, Kate and mostly Johnny and Rosie. And yes, maybe Dianne and me... Thanks for your time. Seriously, thanks for your time... Dave "Pop" Gunnip.

God willing... to be continued...